The LEADERSHIP FACTOR

A Leadership Guide for the Retail Automotive Industry

By

David Lewis

The LEADERSHIP FACTOR

All of the anecdotes included are based on true events. Names, of course, have been changed, and some situations have been combined or slightly fictionalized for clarification and illustration purposes.

ISBN Number: 978-0-615-73116-2

First Edition: January 2013

Published in North America by David Lewis & Associates, Inc.

Printed in the United States of America

TABLE OF CONTENTS

INTRODUCTION

This is a book about Leadership. Not just any kind of Leadership, but Leadership in the retail automotive sales industry. People outside of our business most likely think there is no such thing.

The public opinion of car dealers has for decades been formed by stories told at backyard barbecues about someone who got taken advantage of on their last purchase at the Dealership downtown; or movies where the Used Car Salesperson is depicted as a modern version of the wild west snake oil hustler.

They are the shifty individuals who wear sunglasses, put on a big grin and greets you with a handshake, while the other hand is busy stealing your wallet. Or the F&I person, who sold you the $298 undercoating you didn't really need unless you lived in Michigan, where they salt the roads during the winter. But, you live in Arizona.

Their version of a car Dealership doesn't include Leaders. Just a bunch of con-men trying to outsmart the public with slick ads, small print and a low-ball estimate of how much their trade is really worth. They sit with their feet up on the desk smoking cigars and telling stories about the last sale they hit it big on and the sucker that bought it.

If you've been in the auto business for a while, you know there's some merit to those opinions. If you are still in it today, hopefully you are aware of the revolution that is now taking place in our industry to change all of that. This revolution has to do with a fundamental change that puts the Customer in the passenger seat and where the Dealership is dedicated to meeting and exceeding their expectations.

At the forefront of this change, you will find Leaders pointing the way. These are men and women from every aspect of our trade who recognize the rights that Customers have and the wrongs they have often been subjected to by people unworthy of their business.

As a Motivational and Leadership Trainer in the automotive industry, I have crossed the country and met these new Leaders in Dealerships and seminars, where I have had the privilege of sharing what I learned from my years in auto sales, management and training.

Since 1986, I've been doing what I do, speaking with Owners, Managers, Salespeople and Service personnel from every aspect of the trade. What I've seen has been impressive to say the least.

Over the past several years, the auto industry as a whole has been nearly shipwrecked. Over-regulation, oil prices, and the current economic crisis have hit auto factories and Dealerships like a meteor crashing in from outer space.

Out of the ashes of this crisis, a new vision is being born. It is that vision that inspired me to write this book. And it is the visionary Leaders I've met as I've traveled the country who are forging the way to a new future with great horizons for those who work in this business, and those we serve who make it worth doing.

It's not easy to define Leadership. A brief look in any dictionary will show you what I mean. In fact, Leadership is not a thing, it's an action. It's an action that takes place when those who manage people seek to find excellence in what they do, and then transfer that excellence to others.

As we journey through the land of Leadership, we will see it through the philosophies and actions of those who practice it in the Dealerships of America. I will expose what Leadership is and what it is not, and show how you, and anyone who desires to pursue excellence, can aspire to become a great Leader.

Our world is changing and we must change with it. Technology has skyrocketed us into the future and those who are unwilling to embrace this, will be left behind or find themselves selling a few cars a year from their used tire business.

But like in everything, before real transformation can take place, the people who work in our industry must change. Those who recognize this need for change are stepping up and making a difference wherever they can. From the top down new Leaders are actively forging a better future for the people who serve in automotive sales and service.

A new generation of young men and women looking for a lifetime career are finding great opportunities in our industry. The professionalism and excellence that is being taught and practiced in today's Dealerships offer real hope for those seeking a promising and lucrative profession.

As someone who makes their living serving the Dealership community, I am happy to see this happening. This book is my contribution to that effort.

David Lewis

CHAPTER 1
WHAT IS LEADERSHIP

It's Monday morning and you've arrived at ABC Motors just in time for the eight o'clock sales meeting. The other Salespeople are already here and are busy enjoying the coffee and bagel's while they wait for the Manager's to show up.

You had yesterday off with your family and now it's time to get back to work on that bonus you've been chasing. Only two more sales and you're there.

The white board on the conference room wall is marked with the deals that have already been logged. There are only a couple days left until the end of the month, so there's no time to waste.

You take a quick glance at the sales board and there's your name at the top: 'Mike - 11 new and 5 used.' Wow! Only two more and you're there. You already have that new Chevy Truck going out this afternoon to Mr. & Mrs. Jones. That thousand dollar bonus for hitting eighteen this month is looking pretty possible right now.

The Sales Manager Richard comes in, followed by Ray, the Used Car Manager. Everyone finds their place at the long conference table and takes a seat. There's an air of excitement in the room as they each take a last glance at their numbers for the month to make sure they're on target.

"Good morning guys and gals," says Richard in his usual jovial way. "Sorry I'm a little late. I had something I needed to ask Shirley in the office before the meeting this morning."

"It looks like were closing in on a great month and I just want to tell you all how much I appreciate what you've done so far. I spoke with the Dealer on the phone just a few minutes ago and he wanted me to express his appreciation to all of you for the great job you are all doing. He couldn't be happier with how things are going this month."

"By the way Mike," Richard says, turning to look your way, "I got a call just before I left Saturday on that dealer trade for your delivery this afternoon to Mr. & Mrs. Jones. I wanted to make sure it got here on time so I've already sent Thomas the lot attendant to pick it up

for you. I would have called you yesterday, but I didn't want to bother you during your family time. You're so close to hitting eighteen this month I want to make sure nothing falls through the cracks so you can get your bonus numbers on the board."

"That's great," you reply. "I really appreciate your help on that."

Just then Ray the Used Car Manager chimes in, "Hey Mike, that reminds me. While your Customers were here on Saturday I took a few minutes to look at their trade again and I remembered a couple that came in last month looking for a nice used truck like that. You remember them? Here, I wrote their number down for you. You might want to call them in case they haven't bought anything yet. Selling your Customers trade-in could get you to the bonus money."

"I'll do that right after the meeting Ray," you reply, "Thanks for the heads up."

"By the way," Ray say's, "I thought that maybe we could pull something off so I've already spoken to the Service Department and they are ready to service the trade-in immediately after the Jones's drive off in their new truck. This way if the other folks are still looking for a truck, you could turn it over in a day."

"Good work Ray," says Richard. "That's the way we need to be thinking if we want to make this a big month."

"Way to go Mike!" says another Salesperson. "Looks like you might beat us all this month buddy. And just a few months ago you didn't know if you could even sell cars."

Everybody in the room started hooting and gave a little cheer.

You blush a little with excitement. "This is my first month getting this close. I couldn't have done it without all of you helping me. And you're right Larry. I wasn't sure I could make it as a car Salesman, but working with all of you has been great. I've learned more here in these few months than I ever did working at my last job. Thanks a lot guys. I really mean it."

"Listen up", says Richard the Manager. "The months not over yet and some of you still have time to sell more cars and earn a bonus too. Anything can still happen. Ray and I are here to do whatever we can to help you. I'm not going to spend a lot of time talking this morning since you all know what our goals are. Who has something that they need our help with this morning?"

Stephanie, one of the other sales reps says she has a lease that is pretty close if they could get a little more *for their trade, as the Customer is a bit short on their up-front money. She says, "About $500 more would do it I think."*

Richard replies, "Let me call a few Wholesalers and see what I can do. Maybe I can package their trade with some other cars I need to sell."

"That would be great Richard. What do I need to do?" she asks.

"Why don't you give them a call, tell them we are trying to get a few more dollars for their trade and we should know later in the day"

"I will," says Stephanie. "Look out Mike, I'm still chasing you." She says, glancing your way with a sly smile.

Everyone lets out a little laugh on that one.

"Okay," Richard says, "I think we all know what we need to do. If you are working on something hot this morning, go do that first. Ray and I will come around to each of you and look at your work sheets for this month to see if there's something we can do to help turn some of them into deals by Wednesday night. This is when it's time to look under every stone. We might find something we overlooked."

"By the way," he adds, "I've got a $100 gift card for whoever makes the first sale of the day. And it's got to be something that hasn't already been written up."

A couple of high-fives and everyone gets up and heads for the sales floor.

The above discourse is an example of Leadership in action. Take a moment to go over each step of the meeting we just attended. I can't think of a better way to describe what Leadership is than to demonstrate it through the daily happenings in a Dealership where everyone is working as a single unit.

If you've ever worked in a lot where it's every person for themselves, you can probably appreciate how things work at ABC Motors. The chances of that happening by accident are not very realistic. The teamwork you see there is a result of the dynamic called 'Leadership.'

But what exactly is Leadership?

Giving a simple answer to that question is not an easy task. The common definition of Leadership is the process of guiding others to accomplish their goals. But, as in all things to do with the automotive industry, it's not quite that simple.

Why? Because there are so many interlinking departments and personalities, the definition of Leadership takes on new dimensions when applying it to the automotive trade.

For the sake of simplicity, let me just say that 'Leadership is what Leaders do'. In other words, Leadership is defined by the many facets of what Leaders do in the process of guiding others to accomplish their goals.

I assure you this is not an attempt on my part to avoid clearly defining Leadership. But as we study Leaders in our business, you will see more clearly why I have chosen to define Leadership this way.

If we take a brief look at the sales meeting at ABC Motors we see several things happening: Richard, the Sales Manager, is eager to encourage his team in any way he can. He doesn't do it from the desk only, but interacts with his whole team to keep abreast of what's going on. This enables him to assist them with all the power and knowledge he has to help his staff members. He respects his staff and treats them as professionals.

As the Quarterback of his team, he pulls together the resources of his other Managers and equips them to interact with his sales team and use their skills and knowledge to help them work their deals. The Salespeople are not left to their own devices under a Leader like Richard, he is totally involved, yet without micro-managing the team or doing it for them.

As a strong Leader, Richard knows the value of incentives to motivate the team to go the extra mile. He stands up for them and get's approval from the Dealer to give extra incentives to encourage them to higher levels of performance.

Ray, the Used Car Manager, stays in tune with what the sales force is working on and is looking for ways to bring solutions where he can. By such things as closely evaluating trade-in vehicles and helping connect his Salespeople with possible opportunities they might have overlooked, he shows himself to be a strong Leader in his department.

From the Lot Boy to the Dealership Owner, ABC Motors functions as a single unit, all committed to creating excellence and value for those who come to them looking to purchase their vehicles.

This is teamwork in action, under Leadership that is geared to produce excellence in every aspect of the Dealership as a whole. The chances for success are highly anticipated in this type of organization. They have a clear focus on their goals and objectives and all work closely together to see that they become a reality.

CHAPTER 2
THE FIVE ESSENTIALS OF LEADERSHIP

When I first came into the automotive sales business, I had the privilege of being hired by someone who proved to be a genuine Leader. His guidance and encouragement to me were a vital part of my early success and helped me to excel in both my selling and management careers.

Having now been a Motivational and Sales Trainer in this industry for many years, the principles I learned from my first employer and other Leaders I have known since, still help guide me to excellence and continued success in my life. Through the influence I have experienced from professionals I have met along the way, I have learned to be a better Leader myself to those who work on my staff at David Lewis and Associates. For this, I will always be grateful.

Though there are a variety of Leadership styles in the automotive industry, there are five distinct essentials that I believe apply to all Leaders in general. If any of these are absent in a Leaders philosophy or skills, they will not be as effective as they could be in their efforts to guide others to success. The following are those five essential qualities:

1. Leadership is about influencing others

Everyone in our lives influences us in some way. We form our opinions and attitudes based on the people and things to which we are exposed to throughout our lives. Each of us ultimately becomes who we are through our exposure to the words and actions of those we know and respect, and the other things that influence us on a regular basis.

Leaders know the power they have to affect change and they demonstrate in their daily lives those things which they desire to teach others. It is not enough to say what you want others to do, you must show them, and do so in such a way as to create a desire in them to follow in your path.

If you are a Sales Manager, your commitment to learn and grow in new methods and skills will inspire those you lead to do the same. As technologies and philosophies of selling and team development advance, those who take advantage of this knowledge will have the best chance for success. Your willingness to guide other through their day to day routines and help them grow in their communication and sales skills can make a tremendous difference in their ability to achieve.

As a department Manager, make sure you are transparent and approachable to those who are on your staff. You want to be careful not to micromanage them, but let them know you are always available to help them when they need it. The more they see this in you as their Leader, the more they will become transparent and helpful with you and with other team members. They will follow your lead in such things even when you don't know they are doing so.

The practices and habits you display in your role as a Leader will directly affect your ability to help those you lead. If you are a person of honesty and integrity, those who follow you will be influenced to emulate you in the same way. If you are committed to hard work and excellence, you will encourage them to be the same.

The potential you have as a Leader to influence those you lead can impact them in their business and personal lives, improve the quality and productivity of their work, and better their chances for success.

2. Leadership is a verb and not a noun

A common mistake we often make is to think of a Leader as someone who has a title saying they are the one in charge. But Leadership is best demonstrated through what someone does, not what position they hold in the Dealership. Leadership is a verb inferring action, not a noun signifying a person, place or thing.

Those who view Leadership as a noun, would consider their role as more of a figurehead who demands respect and attention. This type of Leadership never invokes the esteem and loyalty that true Leaders receive from peers and subordinates. Their ability to develop team cooperation and unity is hindered by their need to control and dominate rather than to lead.

As a great Leader you want to be the action word. You want to be the one that makes things happen. That shows others how to act, perform and succeed. Words like lead, guide, demonstrate and follow are all action words, and are thus verbs. You always want those you lead to view you as someone they will follow, someone who they trust to guide them to success.

Leaders act out their roles by going before those they lead, and guiding them in the path of achievement. It is what they do that makes them Leaders and not just the sign on their door or desk. Neither is it the position assigned to them by the Dealership organization. They earn their position of Leadership through the commitment and dedication they show to the success of those they lead. They help them achieve the goals they are reaching for by guiding them through the process of their daily tasks and encouraging and inspiring them each step of the way.

If you want to inspire those you lead to set and accomplish goals, you too must do the same. Let them see how hard you work to accomplish the things you aspire to achieve. Offer clear guidance to help them in their daily routines. Teach them how to keep a written record of their goals. And teach them the difference between short term, long term and daily goals and how they work. Spend time with them going over their goals to make sure they are doing what needs to be done on a daily basis to achieve them.

Your actions as a Leader will best be authenticated by the motivation and success that you impart to those you are leading. When they see you reaching higher and aspiring to excellence as their Leader, they will be inspired to follow you and desire to reach their highest personal potential.

3. Leadership is about creating change and facilitating growth

As a Leader it is your responsibility to continually be creating change and facilitating growth in both your team and organization. This can come in the form of new ideas, better tools or stronger concepts. You must be constantly searching out new ways, and become an avid student of our trade and profession. Guiding someone to do something that is old and outdated will not help them to become successful.

Be innovative and fearless to try things that may be new to you. Find new training resources to bring to the attention of the group and creative ways to work together to help them further develop their knowledge and skills.

If you have someone who is excellent in doing a vehicle walk around, let that person demonstrate the proper methods to the group as a training exercise. Another may have expertise in product knowledge, or in how best to do a meet and greet. All of these can be essential at any time to create success and are important skills for your sales staff.

One of the most effective tools for creating change and growth is the use of role playing. It is not always easy to get seasoned personnel to participate in such activities if they are not already used to doing so. The longer they have been in the business, the harder it can be to get them to take role playing seriously.

Take the lead in such activities yourself. Getting started in role playing is somewhat like doing karaoke. At first, everyone is a bit timid, but after a few, take the lead and step up. Pretty soon everyone wants to sing. Don't be discouraged if it takes a little time to get started. Once they realize that it can be both fun and informative, they will be glad to participate.

There are many such exercises that can benefit the group as a whole and thus advance them in their skills as Salespeople. Such things also help them see how you as their Leader recognize the special skills they possess and that you value their team commitment and individual abilities.

If you are a Service or Parts Manager, encourage your service workers to stay educated in the latest techniques and allow them to participate in training that will advance their skills. Do your best to make sure they have the necessary tools, equipment and parts inventory to carry out their tasks. Let them know how much you appreciate their professionalism with incentives and special recognition awards for the work they do.

Often, Service personnel tend to be more isolated because they work in their own space throughout the day performing a specialized skill. In a busy Dealership, this can put a lot of pressure on them to perform in a time frame that keeps them so busy they have little time for interaction. Take the time to find creative ways to develop a spirit of teamwork among those under your Leadership, as well as with other departments within your Dealership.

Let your Service Writers and Manager's alternate being the contact person when someone in sales needs to do a Customer service walk. This can help them learn to communicate with Customers and to introduce special offerings and benefits you provide to those who come in for service. This also helps them to keep in touch with the various aspects of the business and to recognize the connection between departments, and how the Dealership functions as one unit.

4. Leadership deals with people and their dynamics

The more you work with people, the more you realize the uniqueness each one has in their own way. As a Leader, it is critical to learn how to understand those you lead and how best to help them grow in their individual skills and natural talents in order to function at their highest potential.

People have different personalities and it is important to understand what drives those who work for you. Your ability to help guide them to more success will often depend upon your knowledge of their basic motivations and the desires they have for their life and career. Spend time with them and learn about their personal lives and their goals for their family and their future. What do they want to achieve? Unless you know, you cannot help them get there. Unless you ask, you will never know.

Everybody is different. They are motivated differently, react differently to coaching and require different levels of attention to help them reach their goals. Once you know what they are trying to achieve, and learn about their basic natural abilities and motivations, you can help them construct a plan for achieving success.

Leadership also requires that you be flexible in your own personality as well. How you deal with groups of people will be different than how you deal with them one on one. It is very important that you always have your Leadership hat on and be confident in your own abilities.

The perfect candidate allows you to lead them and how you interact with those people, will be different than how you interact with those who do not. Some are going to resent you, and some will even try to make you fail and try to de-throne you as their Leader. You cannot let those negative people or thoughts determine how you deal with them.

The most important thing is for you to stay focused on your Leadership role. Never drop down to their levels. Show them that no matter how they react to you, and your role as their Leader, you are still going to treat them with dignity and respect.

5. Leadership is about advancing others

True Leaders find their success in the achievements of those they lead. If those you lead come to believe that your goals are for your own personal advancement, your Leadership will come to an end. You must never forget that your rewards come solely from the achievements of others. The more you help them to achieve their objectives, the more your position as Leader will be established and fortified.

Every time you speak with your staff, whether as a group or as individuals, your entire focus must be as follows:

- **What is best for them**

- **What will make them more successful**

- **How they can best achieve their wants and needs**

Avoid mentioning your success, your failures, your goals or desires and only speak of theirs. Try to refrain from talking about the Dealerships goals, the Dealer's expectations or how successful other Dealerships are. This only turns the spotlight away from them and onto you or someone else.

The more you place the focus on their goals and how to achieve them, the more they will come to view you as someone who has their best interest at heart. Your job as their Leader is to influence them, help them change their bad habits, develop good habits, and ultimately reach their goals.

Once you make your Leadership role all about them, you will see those you lead listen more intently, follow your directions more clearly, and start to see results they did not experience before. When this happens they will give you permission to lead them and your ability to coach them to success will increase tremendously.

CHAPTER 3
WHAT A PERSON MUST KNOW ABOUT THEIR LEADER

If you have been around the business a while, you probably remember the Glory Days of Selling. Those were times when buyers rarely questioned the quality of your product. Business was booming, and a Sales Managers primary qualification was based solely on how many vehicles they could move every month.

Times have changed, and for the retail auto industry to flourish, we have to change with them. The old adage "If it ain't broke don't fix it," doesn't work any longer. Automobile Dealerships are now restructuring from the top down. Terms like Rebranding, Image Consulting and Independent Business Coaching have found their way into what once was an industry that operated on a 'business as usual' basis.

In today's Dealerships, highly respected Leaders are introducing new ideas and concepts designed to meet and exceed Customer requirements. Today's buyer has expectations of product quality, fuel economy, long term dependability and competitive pricing. They come to your Dealership with computer printouts of product and pricing information tucked under their arms and they want to be treated with respect and fairness.

To thrive in this changing environment, Dealers and Managers today must provide new models of Leadership that take full advantage of the innovations now taking place in business philosophies and strategies. At the heart of these innovative methods is the concept of Team Development.

For those in Management, this becomes particularly challenging. Building a team that can win the business of today's demanding Customers is not easy from any perspective. Innovative Leaders must interact directly with their staff in order to create the trust and confidence that will allow them to lead the way for great success. Just as the Customers' business must be earned, so must the status of Leader be earned from those you lead.

In order to do this, you must get to know your staff and they must know you. Your transparency and professionalism must be apparent to them at all times. You must be prepared to make their goals and success the priority of your job as their Leader.

But what things do those you supervise want to know about you as their Leader? What must you demonstrate to them that will inspire them to follow your Leadership to achieve the success they are seeking?

➢ Those you lead must know what your goals are

The first item on the list is your goals. The late Henry Ford once said, "Obstacles are those frightful things you see when you take your eyes off your goal."

Until those you lead know your goals, they will only see the obstacles that are in front of them resisting their efforts for success. Until they understand what your goals are, they cannot know how their own aspirations fit into the scheme of your Leadership. What are your short and long term goals? What goals do you expect them to reach? And how will you lead them to achieve these things?

Those you lead want to know your personal business goals. If you are a Sales Manager, do you want to be a General Manager? If you are a General Manager, do you want to someday own your own Dealership? If you are the Dealer, are you planning to open more Dealerships? Knowing this will enable them to see their own future through your goals and help them find value in the loyalty and growth you expect from them.

True professionals want to make sure they share those same desires for success. They want to be associated with someone who has clear goals and strategies for continued growth and development.

In my early days as a Salesperson I had a Sales Manager that only had one goal we shared in common, and that was to sell cars. Yet he set the same target every month for volume. His goal every month was to sell eighty cars.

Most months we reached that goal, yet he never raised the bar any higher. He would only lower the goal at certain times of the year, like December or January. He had no ambitions to be anything more than a Sales Manager. He was content with his yearly earnings and his job performance.

I personally had trouble viewing him as my Leader. Sure he was my Sales Manager, and I did what he asked of me, but I never looked at him as anything more and clearly not as someone I could follow. Where would I follow him to? In my mind he wasn't going anywhere.

If I were still working for him, he would probably still be the Sales Manager (if the Dealership even survived until now) and I would still be a Salesperson. As my Leader I wanted him to guide me to the next level in my career. How could he do that when he himself was satisfied with selling eighty cars a month and had no apparent ambitions to grow?

Keep in mind, not everybody is going to agree with your goals. Some might think they are too ambitious, while others may consider them inadequate. Nevertheless, those you lead want to know you have them. Be sure your goals are always out there for your team to see and that you are constantly trying to achieve them. Once you do achieve them, keep raising the bar to inspire them to do the likewise.

➤ Those you lead must know your ambitions

The next thing your team wants to know about you as their Leader is what your ambitions are. Though you may think goals and ambitions are the same, they are not. A goal is a tangible target that you strive to achieve. It has a time frame or an expiration date. Ambitions are far reaching and go beyond goals as the pinnacle of what you desire to achieve.

As a Sales Manager, your goal might be to deliver 150 cars this month, or to generate $200,000 in revenue. Your goal is defined by the 150 cars or $200,000 and has a time frame or expiration date which is the end of the month. When you have done this, you have successfully accomplished your goal.

An ambition on the other hand can be defined in one of four ways. First, it is an earnest desire for some type of achievement or distinction, such as power, honor, fame or wealth and requires a willingness to strive for its attainment. For example, someone may have the ambition to someday become the President of the United States. To do this there are certain goals that must be set and reached along the way if they are to have any chance of success.

Ambition can also be defined as a desire for work or activity. For example, 'I awoke feeling tired and utterly lacking ambition.' In this definition, ambition is affected by physical or emotional status and represents more of a temporary mental or physical condition.

Ambition can also be a state of achievement, a result desired, or something sought after. For example, 'Becoming President of the United States, was his only ambition in life.'

Finally, and probably the most common definition for most of us, is that our ambition demonstrates our desire for success, achievement or distinction. Something we aspire to obtain or accomplish that has no specific deadline.

In our business, some examples might be your desire to have an elite sales force, or to have your own Dealership one day. Those are both attainable ambitions, yet you have not put any defined deadline or expiration date as to when you would like to achieve them.

As a Leader it is important that you clearly differentiate between your goals and ambitions. Once you put a deadline or expiration date on your ambitions, they then become goals. If you share your ambitions and do not achieve them, then many think you have failed. Failing an ambition is unacceptable. For this reason you have to make sure your goals and ambitions are kept in check, and that your goals can ultimately lead you to achieve your ambitions.

➢ Those you lead want to know your background

The next bit of information that is important to those who you lead will be your background. Where do you come from, and what have you done that should make them accept you as their Leader?

When the word background is mentioned many of us think about ones' education. From a formal sense that often means where did you go to school and what level have you obtained in your learning, such as degrees or certifications?

Obviously, if you are the Office Manager or Controller in your Dealership, your formal education would be very important – where you went to college and what is your degree in? Or if you are a Mechanic, what technical school did you get your training from and what level of certification have you acquired?

For a Sales Manager, General Manager or Dealer your formal education is not as critical. It is normal for Leaders in these departments to rise up through the ranks as they excel in their sales career.

What is critical for any position of Leadership is how you arrived at the position you now hold. Where have you worked in the past? What experience do you have? And who has provided you with that experience?

If you are a Sales Manager how many cars did you sell a month? How were your grosses? And why were you promoted? I have met many Sales Managers that had only been Salespeople for a year or less. Obviously they had developed some great skill levels to be promoted so fast. So, what are they?

If you have only been in the industry for five years and have already reached the level of General Manager, tell me about your success as a Salesperson and Sales Manager, and what made it possible for you to achieve the level of GM so fast. Why is this important to me as a member of you team? Because if you did it so fast I want to do it that fast too! I want to learn from someone who can show me, teach me, and lead me to that same level!

As a Leader you hold a position that is often sought after by others. Remember, it is much easier for you to go to the next level yourself, if you have someone on your team who you have led to successfully take your place. That is one of the true signs of a great Leader: the ability to develop their staff to move into their position at some point in time.

If your progression to your current position took time, then share with those you lead how you learned those things that helped you progress to get there. Explain what goals you achieved in order to be promoted to the next level and the steps you took in order reach those goals.

People love success stories! Because most want to be a success story themselves, your ability to effectively share the stages of your progress can help them set goals for paving their own career path.

➢ Those you lead must know your strengths and weaknesses

Next on the list is probably the most difficult aspect of what those you lead must know in order to follow you as their Leader. They must know your strengths and weaknesses, and that you are willing to be transparent in your position as Leader.

There is a reason why you have become, or are in the process of becoming a Leader in your Dealership. It is because those above you in the organization who promoted or hired you recognize that you are good at what you do.

As the General Manager, you obviously possess strong business and people skills. If you are the Service Manager, you clearly have a strong working knowledge of how cars operate and the ins and outs of running a Service Department. And if you are a Sales Manager, you know how to help negotiate and close deals.

All great Leaders realize that, in general, they are extremely competent and good at what they do. They also recognize certain areas in which they excel more than others.

For example, with me, my strengths have always been in closing. I can pencil a deal, coach a salesperson through the process, and guide them through to a successful delivery. I also know how to order cars, arrange the lot for the best exposure of our product and create some simple advertising campaigns. But, my greatest strength is in closing deals.

I want those that I lead to know that. I want them to know that not only am I good at it, but that I love doing it. How else could I teach them to be successful closers if I myself were incompetent in this? My proven success makes me confident in this area of my Leadership.

However, in other things I recognize that I am not as strong as some others on my team that may have more experience in certain areas. Being a Leader does not mean that I am the best at everything, it just means I know where to find the solutions when they are required.

It was said of Henry Ford that late in his life his ability to lead the Ford Motor Company came into question when he failed to answer well during a court examination concerning his competence. The judge commented that if the aging Mr. Ford could not answer such simple questions, how could he be expected to continue as the head of such a large company?

Supposedly Mr. Ford responded that he didn't need to know those things himself. He had on his desk a row of buttons he could push that would immediately bring any of several people in who could answer those questions for him. On that note the case was dismissed.

Whether this story is true or not it certainly demonstrates the fact that successful Leaders don't need to know everything. They just need to know where to find the answers that will allow them to get the job done.

Don't be fearful of what you do not excel at. We cannot all be good at everything. If you are stronger at closing than at advertising, let someone else handle the advertising if you have a staff member who is better at it than you. Play into your strengths and away from your weaknesses.

Now, I am not endorsing the idea that you give up on your weaknesses. Keep working on those areas, and keep searching out help or expertise. People respect someone who realizes their own weaknesses, yet still continues to find ways to improve. This truly shows your Leadership commitment to both your organization and those you lead.

The point I am trying to make is this, be proud of what you do best, and let those you lead know these are your strengths. Make them aware that they can come to you if they need your expertise in any particular area.

Leadership is a supportive role. Be proactive with your strengths, but whenever possible allow other to assist in areas where they have more experience. Find creative ways to allow those who are exceptional in certain areas to be recognized for their special abilities. Put them out front when you want to train other team members to develop certain strengths and skills. This will only fortify your position as a strong Leader.

CHAPTER 4
THREE TYPES OF SUPERVISORS

Working in the retail automotive industry is one of the most promising and unique career opportunities in America today. And it has been so since it began in the early 20th Century. Where else can someone starting with no experience, little product knowledge and limited education make the kind of money that can be made by those who learn to do this business well?

Most of those who sit in positions of Leadership in our industry came up through the ranks. Some of today's most successful Dealership owners got their start working on a car lot as sales or service personnel with little or no previous experience. Eventually, they worked their way up through the ranks to become Dealers, owning their own successful business or even chains of Dealerships.

Though it is important to look behind us and remember where we came from, it is even more critical that we look ahead to see where we are going. Innovators in today's automobile sales and service marketplace recognize that everything must be transformed if we are to have continued success in this fast changing world of technology and information. We can no longer rely upon business structures and methods that formed the basis for our success in the past. We must be prepared to take up the challenges that face us if we are to retain our status as an essential part of the American Dream.

With the advancement of new business philosophies and methods for sales and service, there is a growing need for those who will step up and fill the roles of supervisors and managers. As the needs and wants of our Customers have evolved, so must the abilities of those who serve them. In many ways our success or failure will depend upon the quality of Leaders that run the various departments in our Dealerships today and into the future.

Quality supervision is critical to the success of any organization that employs people. The challenge of finding reliable and inspired Leaders who can guide the retail automotive industry forward has never been greater than it is today. As the face of business changes, we must change with it. Our success to do so will depend largely upon the value our Dealership organizations place on those they choose to manage the people who work there.

In every business there must be those who oversee and direct others to make certain they are doing their jobs in a way that will accomplish the goals and objectives of the company. Without Supervisors, there would be little organization, and people would just go about their daily tasks doing as they pleased with no guidance, direction or accountability. It would be complete and utter anarchy. It is the job of a supervisor to hold it all together and bring order to the chaos of total independence among the workforce.

Being a Supervisor can be very rewarding mentally, physically and monetarily. It can also be a very demanding position with lots of pressure and stress. For some, being a Supervisor entails more responsibility than they are willing to take on and they would rather work for less money than to carry the weight of such a position. The diversity and stress of overseeing others does not appeal to everyone. Some prefer to focus on their own work, and find their fulfillment in being the best they can be at what they do.

There are three basic types of supervisors managing our Dealerships today, and the way they function in their roles will ultimately determine the level of success their organization attains. They are *Bosses*, *Managers*, and *Leaders*. Each one of these supervisor types operate in their own unique fashion. The way they view their role will determine the results and the respect they receive from those they supervise.

➢ The Boss Type

On the bottom rung of the totem pole is the Boss. This type of individual sees their role as telling others what to do and ordering their workers around in a bullish manner. They leave little or no room for discussion and will not tolerate any opinions other than their own as to how things should be done. With the Boss it's always, "My way or the highway."

Bosses rule by intimidation and the authority which their position grants them. Those who work under this type of Leadership are reluctant to do anything that would cost them their job, so they set creativity and personal growth aside and just do what they're told. This breeds an environment that rewards loyalty over productivity and hinders teamwork among the staff.

Bosses require strict guidelines and rarely, if ever, operate outside of the box. They are intelligent people who know how to get the job done, but they are self-focused and operate from a mindset of career survival and Leadership by rank. They do not function well in a team environment and prefer to work beneath upper management, but over the workforce.

➢ The Manager Type

Next up the ladder of supervisory roles is the Manager. This type of person operates from the premise of efficiency and structure. They guide those under them with a stern posture and rely upon the direction that comes from above to provide goals and objectives to their staff.

Unlike the Boss, the Manager can be very good at laying out direction and setting goals, but they lack creativity and rely primarily on repeating the processes that have worked in the past. They are not bully types, but they expect full cooperation from those they supervise in order to give a good report to the organization about how they are fulfilling their duties.

Managers know how to organize a task and how to explain it to others, but they work in an isolated environment preferring to use formulas, processes and directives rather than to interact with their team members on a one to one basis. Their loyalty is to the organizational objectives rather than to the individual goals of their staff. They justify their position by past successes that they had before they became Manager.

In the retail automotive business, the term Manager is used for almost every Department Head. But, for those who are in the trade that doesn't necessarily signify Leadership or productivity. It is more a part of a hierarchical structure that has been in place for many decades. I will discuss this more as I share the individual traits of each supervisory role and how they fulfill the position they hold in their organization.

➢ The Leader Type

Our final supervisory type is the Leader. This individual inspires others to perform and to grow in their abilities and potential. They produce results that are based upon the achievement of specific objectives and their employees follow them because they share a common goal. They measure their own achievements by the success of those they lead and are not self-serving in any way.

The role of a Leader is one that sets people free to accomplish whatever their gifts and abilities can achieve. They empower their workers to learn and grow, and set the example for them by their own continuous search for knowledge and innovation. They lead by inspiration, not by perspiration, yet they are tireless in the pursuit of success for those who work with them.

The role of Leader is one that all those who supervise others should aspire to. Once achieved, the pressures of work are reduced and stress is minimized for them, as well as for those they oversee. They develop a following among their staff members because they function as a role model or mentor to those who work for them. They see themselves as a part of their team and devote themselves to advancing all of their employees to higher levels of success and productivity

As we delve deeper into these three types of supervisory roles you will see that all who take a Leadership position start out in the eyes of those under them as a Boss. Then, if they do their job properly, they progress into becoming a Manager. Finally, those who dedicate themselves to excellence and the study of team building will eventually become Leaders.

Becoming a Leader to those you supervise is something that must be earned. Though you may have the title of Manager, it does not necessarily mean you are functioning in the role as it is perceived by those you manage. A Leader must earn the respect of those they supervise before they will be recognized by them as their Leader.

Of course,one of the perils of being a Leader is the looming potential of sliding back down to the level of Manager or Boss. It is always easier to slide down a ladder then it was to climb up it. Once you achieve the position and role of Leader among your staff, you must work hard to advance yourself in knowledge, and take advantage of the vast storehouse of training resources available today to help you in your task.

Leaders must devote themselves to the pursuit of excellence, and acquire any training and knowledge that will help them lead their team members to achieve. By doing so, they ensure their own future and advance those in their charge to higher levels on the ladder of success.

So right now, determine where you are on that ladder. Are you a Boss? Are you a Manager? Or are you already a Leader? Only your staff can tell you who you are. Don't be afraid to find out. To do so is the beginning of your journey to the top of your career. Perception is reality and how those you supervise perceive you will decide if and how they will follow you as their Leader.

The more you progress in your abilities and development as a Leader, the easier it will become to create a path of success for yourself and for those who work under your Leadership. As we look more closely at the individual roles of Boss, Manager, and Leader make a good assessment of where you are and what you need to do to move up and take your position as a strong Leader in your organization.

CHAPTER 5
CHARACTERISTICS OF A BOSS

Now that I have shared with you the three types of Supervisors, I want to break down into more detail the characteristics of each entity, beginning with a Boss. After that I will focus on the Manager, and finally the characteristics of a Leader.

If anyone understood the value of Leadership in his day it was former President Theodore Roosevelt. He was a man's man, and he knew how to inspire those around him to achieve victory. He once said, *"People ask the difference between a Leader and a Boss. A Leader leads and a Boss drives."*

If you've been in the retail auto trade for a while, Mr. Roosevelt's words may bring to mind a Boss you have worked for in the past. Every day you were reminded of how little you were doing and what was expected of you. Motivation came in the form of criticism and every month, the fear of losing your job, if you were not producing, made you view Customers as marks to be taken rather than a client to be served.

Under this type of supervision, the end of the month sales meeting usually started with a bang and ended with the statement, *"Well that was good. But what are you going to do for me now? If you don't sell more cars this month, we may all lose our jobs."* Fifteen minutes of glory, a few kudos, and then on to the next cattle drive. And we were the cattle being driven.

Though I'm aware that there are still many Dealerships where this type of scene is replayed on a monthly basis, this is a good example of a team that is being driven rather than inspired and guided. Moving away from this format is not easy and requires a lot of commitment from those who are looking for a better way of doing business.

Hopefully, things have changed for those of you who are reading this and are still working in the trade. And if you have just started your career in the automotive industry, my sincere desire is that you are part of a flourishing team being guided by a Leader who has a clear vision for growth and success.

If you are that Leader, I want to applaud you for being an inspiration to those who look to you for training and guidance, and for helping your team members achieve excellence in their work and careers. You, and others like you, are what make this a great business to be in.

As we work through the concepts of great Leadership, it is important to recognize that change and growth constantly take place in and through a true Leader. A Leader's action is like fertilizer to a garden. Their team is the ground they plant and their Leadership is what makes the plant grow.

A Boss thinks differently. Their mind is only on the task at hand. This is especially true if they work for another Boss or a Manager type. They merely pass on to their workers what is being handed down to them, and they expect them to do what they are told in order to finish the task.

Always remember, a Leader leads and a Boss controls!

Those who supervise in this way will settle for the status quo from their employees. To them, their team is just the people who work under them that they supervise. They only implement real change if someone above them requires that they do so. Their focus is on the process rather than the outcome. If everyone just does what they have always done, things will keep working as they should.

Uninspired Leadership like this cannot move things forward and is reminiscent of a factory floor operation in an assembly line. The only thing that matters is the production quota for the month and the Boss keeps the workers moving by reminding them who's in charge.

Please understand that I am not trying to paint Bosses as bad people. We all do what we have learned from those who influenced us along our path. This type of supervisor is just repeating what they were taught by someone else. Unless they are instructed by upper management to change, or are awakened to new Leadership methods through a training program like ours, they will very likely continue doing as they have always done.

In the past, the Dealership was a perfect place where this style of Leadership could be found. The mindset was just to sell to a monthly quota, and Salespeople often moved in and out of favor with the Boss depending on how many units they sold that month. In this environment teamwork was rare because fear of loss was the main motivating factor and you could go from hero to zero every thirty days. If you were having a bad month as a Salesperson, you were constantly reminded about it and often compared to someone who was having a great month.

Bosses who work this way are not typically team players. This would call for more employee interaction than they are prepared to give. They are only interested in themselves, their goals, their advancement and their income, and they view their job through the narrow window of processes and repetition. They do what is required of them and never anything more. And they will often refer back to their own past successes in order to intimidate others by making them feel they are not pulling their weight.

True Leaders never use intimidation. They share their own success stories with their staff only to reinforce the potential that lies within each of them. If someone is having a bad month it doesn't signal their demise, it just creates an opportunity for learning and growth by interaction and input from their Leader and other team members.

A Boss keeps the upper hand by not allowing teammates to have input. To them, an employee's job is to do what they're told and nothing else. They do not work well with others; whether it is those they supervise or other department heads on the same level with them. This often keeps them isolated, except when they have to interact with their workers to make a correction or give an order.

In the sales department, this can manifest itself in many ways. When a Salesperson has been with a Customer working toward closing a sale, they often feel they have a good understanding of what the person wants and what they will respond to. When they take an offer to the desk, if the Boss does not respect the Salesperson's input, they can send them back to the Customer with unacceptable terms and no room for negotiation. This can of course make the Salesperson look powerless and bring a quick end to a potential sale. Because the Salesperson has no authority to negotiate they can only deliver the Boss's terms and the Customer walks. You can grind through a lot of potential buyers this way before making a sale.

Authority is the key to success for the Boss. Having a title is very important to them and they want everyone to know that they are the one in charge of things. They run their department with fear management and a *do it or else* attitude. They are proud of their achievements and often see their success being the result of their ability to run a tight ship. Because of this they don't want their employees to go around them in any way, nor will they tolerate other managers going directly to their workers without first talking to them. If that does happen they want to know why, and they make it clear that they don't like it.

On the flipside of all this, it must be said that Bosses are usually very intelligent and goal oriented people. They know their job and their responsibilities and they usually reach their goals. At the same time, they have a high turnover of staff because of the stress they create in the work environment. The tension of working under a Boss makes going to work a burden rather than something to look forward to.

This type of Leader has a difficult time attracting and hiring talented people and gets a reputation for their harsh style of management. This happens a lot in our business because so many people move from Dealership to Dealership and tell stories about their previous employer. Those who have a plan for developing a growing career and advancing in the industry won't do well with the Boss. They will be seen as competition and as someone eventually wanting to have their job.

As I travel to Dealerships around America, I have opportunity to meet every type of manager. In my training sessions, I often meet people who lead their sales and service force in this way. They have little respect for their staff members and rarely do their staff members respect them. If I speak to their workers, I often find that they do not like or admire their Boss. They respect the position that they hold and the level of success they have achieved, but they are clearly someone they would never choose to follow.

Ironically, most of us think we are Leaders, but most are far from it. If you possess any of these characteristics that I just shared with you, then you are still a Boss. Take a close look at yourself and if you have any of these characteristics, take the time to work on changing them. It can only be a positive change for you, your team and for everyone's future.

Scenario

Sometimes, working for a Boss can be a real challenge no matter what you do. Take Tina as an example, a young lady who works in the Internet Sales Department at her Dealership. She spends a lot of time calling and following up on potential Customers who make contact through the Dealerships new website. She is very diligent and has an impeccable work ethic.

Her Sales Manager doesn't think selling on the Internet is a good idea, but the Dealer paid for an updated website, hired Tina to work in the department and even paid for her training. Unfortunately, the Sale Manager is not sold on internet sales because he thinks people want to smell that new car smell before they buy and you can't do that on the Internet, plus he is under the impression that grosses are always low because the Customer can easily shop Dealership to Dealership online, and finally he thinks it is just a fad that won't last long.

The other day she started working a deal for a Customer that had contacted her through the website. After numerous emails and phone conversations she made an appointment for the Customers to see and drive the car they were interested in. They were very excited about Tina's description of the vehicle and its value, and thus arrived earlier than the appointment time, but Tina wasn't due to come in for a few more hours.

They asked for Tina when they arrived at the Dealership, but her Boss, the Sales Manager, turned the Customer over to another Salesperson. Which, on the surface makes logical sense, but Tina lives only two miles away from the Dealership and had always left clear instructions to call her if a Customer of hers showed up unexpectedly.

In spite of this, the deal was completed and she didn't even know it until she called the Customers later in the day to find out why they hadn't kept their appointment. The Customer then told her they had already arrived early, that they were informed that she was not in yet and that they had purchased the car from another Salesperson, but were told by the Sales Manager that she would have gotten credit for the sale regardless.

Tina complained to the Sales Manager again restating that she only lived two miles away and had always stated she could be contacted and would come right over if a Customer showed up unexpectedly, but he told her it wasn't his responsibility to make sure she was there when her Customers came in. She lost a good commission and having the deal on the board in her name. But to compensate her just a bit the Sales Manager had the other Salesperson give Tina $50 from the deal.

Things like this have happened to her several times under this Sales Manager. When she questions him his answer is always something like: "I run this Department my way. Don't blame me if you can't make your Customers get here on their scheduled time." or "If you don't like the way I run this Dealership there are always other Dealerships you can work at."

This is clearly the characteristic of a Boss. He will never build loyalty or integrity in his department, because he doesn't have any himself. He stands on his authority and anyone who wants to argue with that can go somewhere else to work. He doesn't like the idea of selling on the Internet or having to do things different from the way they've always been done, so he doesn't.

He subscribes to the philosophy of his way or the highway. He is not open to new suggestions, new ideas or new concepts. This Sales Manager will always struggle to find good talented people, will lose the ones he does have to a competitor and will always struggle each month to meet the Dealerships goals.

A strong Leader would have open mindedly embraced the idea of an Internet Department, even if they were not fully sold on the idea. They would have engaged themselves in the training to learn as much as they could about it, supported their hired staff with all their efforts and demonstrated a true want for the department's success.

If he was a true Leader he would have called Tina when her Customer had arrived early, not only to benefit Tina, but to benefit the Customer. Maybe the Customer would have felt more comfortable with Tina and thus the gross would have been higher.

Had he not been able to reach her he would have still assigned it to another Salesperson, but under the premises that it was Tina's deal and that the other Salesperson was just helping out a fellow Salesperson.

Whether you believe in a concept or idea yourself does not matter when it comes to Leadership, as Leadership is about those you lead, and not about your thoughts or beliefs. The Sales Manager in this scenario is a Boss, and without the proper Leadership training will remain a Boss for his entire career.

What are you?

CHAPTER 6 CHARACTERISTICS OF A MANAGER

As we move from the Boss to the next supervisory role of Manager, we will see some similar characteristics, but a marked difference in priority and style. The first attribute I want to examine is the respect that the Manager has.

➢ Managers are respected but only based on past accomplishments

Unlike the Boss, the Manager has the respect of their team, but it is based solely on past performance. They may have done so well in their previous position that promotion seemed like the right thing to those in upper management, so they were made a Manager.

If they have earned the respect of their co-workers while working in sales, it will not likely change immediately in their new position as Manager. But that will only last for a while, as respect that is based upon former accomplishments will only last for a short time.

Many Managers who are promoted up from sales positions often go on to become tremendous Leaders. But, how often have we seen a great Salesperson that regularly produced big numbers every month fail miserably when placed in the position of Manager? Why is that? Doesn't being promoted to the position of Manager prove that you are obviously a Leader? Not necessarily.

The skills required to manage a group of Salespeople are quite different from those required to sell successfully. A manager who does not develop the Leadership skills required for running and advancing an effective sales force will rely upon the same methods they used in sales to produce results in their new position as Manager.

Consider Tom who worked as a Salesperson in a Chevrolet Dealership for over five years. When he first took the position in sales, he came into the business with no experience, but he had a very friendly manner and Customers liked him. Travis, one of the sales veterans at this Dealership, also liked Tom and took him under his wing to help him learn the trade. Within a few short months Tom began to produce good numbers, eventually becoming a top Salesperson in the Dealership.

During his fifth year as a Salesman, the Used Car Manager position came available and Tom was promoted. He moved from his desk on the sales floor to a private office and began to take on the duties of his new position. He started appraising the vehicles that were being traded, and began going to the auctions to buy and sell cars for the Dealership. He learned how to order inventory and do the paperwork that went along with being a Manager.

The General Sales Manager at the Dealership was the owner's son and was familiar with all of the business aspects of ordering inventory, working with banks, advertising, hiring, etc. He had never worked in sales so he always let the sales team do what they did. As long as they met the monthly quota of units sold he was happy. He taught Tom what he knew about working the auctions, appraising trade-ins and doing the necessary paperwork that had to be done every month to keep his department running.

Whenever Tom had a chance, he would sit with the Salespeople and talk about what it was like being a Manager. They all respected what he had accomplished in sales and thought he would probably do well in his new position. As for Tom, he still felt more comfortable with the sales team and was not quite used to working with upper management yet.

If a Salesperson needed some help on a deal Tom was glad to step in. Rather than just assist the Salesperson with the Customer though, he would usually go on and close the sale if he could. He did that quite often and when it happened his friendly personality would kick in and he would connect well with the Customer.

Often that Customer would return to the Dealership looking for another vehicle or to bring in a referral and would want to work directly with Tom. Instead of turning those over to a Salesperson, Tom would usually work the deal himself. He would eventually bring the original Salesperson in after the numbers were worked out and then put the sale under their name for the commission.

Whenever any of Tom's old Customers came in to buy another vehicle he would just write up the deal himself and let a Salesperson make the delivery. He would give them a flat fee and credit for the unit, but not the regular commission. He felt this was fair since he made the sale and the buyers were his previous Customers.

Sometimes the pressure of working these extra deals interfered with his increasing duties as a Manager and if a Salesperson needed help he would often say something like, *"Haven't you learned how to close yet? If I have to work the deal for you why should you get the commission?"*

Eventually, the sales team didn't like letting their Customers talk directly with Tom. They would go around him to work with another Manager if they needed help on a deal. Even Travis, who had mentored Tom as a Salesman, avoided working with him now that he was Manager.

Tom soon lost the respect he once had from the sales team and spent most of his time working inventory in his office or buying and selling at the auctions. He missed the fun and recognition he had as a Salesperson, but didn't want to go backwards. His time was now spent mostly managing paperwork and going to the auctions rather than working with the sales team.

Tom's predicament is not an uncommon one. He once had an exciting career in sales because he worked hard to develop the skills and attitude that it took to become successful. He also had the help of Travis who was a highly experienced Salesperson.

There was no real training program for managers in his Dealership so Tom soon found himself stuck in his new position with no real guidance or coaching. He didn't want to go backwards in his career, but was unsure of how to go forward into Leadership. He often thought to himself, "These things always worked for me in sales. Why aren't they working now?"

Tom will probably survive as a Manager if sales and profits don't decrease substantially under his supervision, and as long as the sales force doesn't change. But if new experienced Salespeople get hired they might wonder how Tom ever became the Manager.

What was lacking in Tom's new career as a Manager was Leadership. Not only his own, but Leadership from those who were above him in the Dealership. He needed to develop different skills to become effective in his new position as Manager. As eager as he was to learn and grow, without someone guiding him in the right way he soon fell into the status quo management style of the Dealership.

There are many Tom's out there who are in positions over their head and don't know how to get where they want to go. Without the proper training and knowledge they will usually end up fulfilling the role of Manager, but never becoming the real Leader that could make a big difference for themselves, the Dealership and for those who work under their supervision.

Tom still has respect in the Dealership, but it has now shifted from those who knew him as an exceptional Salesperson to those who have more to do with the administrative duties of the business. He has become a

Manager type and his focus is much more on efficiency and structure, rather than on strong Leadership.

➢ Managers are trusted

Besides respect, trust is another character trait that Managers usually possess. Whether Dealership owners run a hands-on or hands-off operation, they rely heavily upon their management team. In either case, trust is critical. A Managers trust is something that is usually earned through hard work, devotion to duty and efficiency.

Managers appreciate the company's trust and they work hard to maintain it. For this type of supervisor, the fact that they are trusted, can either empower or hinder their ability to make the changes required for innovation and forward advancement.

Trust can empower the Manager who has confidence to stretch his or her Leadership skills and develop their team's abilities. Yet that same trust can hinder those who are afraid to try new things for fear of losing their position. The step from Manager to Leader always involves taking some risks and not all are willing to do that with their job security.

Like Tom eventually did, a Manager may spend much of their workday dealing with paperwork, ordering cars, inventory reports etc. They can usually set goals and accomplish them, and can deal effectively with problems and situations as they occur. They are efficient at what they do, but often lack the foresight to see problems coming before they arrive. In most cases, the squeaky wheel gets the oil.

Managers encourage quality and goal setting, but rarely provide the Leadership and team interaction that inspires and equips others for great success. As a trusted employee the Manager is already half way there. Trust infers values like honesty, integrity and quality. It does not guarantee success, but it is a major ingredient.

➢ Managers are loyal to the organization not to their staff

A Manager cannot always make the necessary improvements that a true Leader can because they are primarily loyal to the organization. Only when they develop and implement quality Leadership, can this be accomplished. Loyalty to the organization is commendable, but if a Manager's loyalty is only there and not to the staff, their ability to effectively lead and produce other Leaders will fall short.

From the standpoint of job security, being loyal to the organization as a Manager can be a self-protective mechanism and may seem wise. But often the organization has no idea of what makes a successful sales or service team. And loyalty may go up, but it doesn't necessarily come down. A company's survival depends upon bottom line profits. No matter how loyal the Manager may be to the organization, if these wane or become stagnant, he or she will eventually be looking for another job.

Managers who will lead the way in today's stressed economy and multi-faceted Dealership models must have the ability and permission to interface with the Dealerships team from the top to the bottom.

➢ Managers are smart but not independent in their thinking

A strong Leader must be independently creative and think outside the box. This is not always easy for the Manager type. They feel safe following the organizational methods and plans, and are not independent enough to risk their security on their own plan of action. Nor does a Manager feel the need to be independently creative. "I'm loyal and work hard for the company," they might think to themselves. "If they know what they are doing and I carry out their business plan, it's not my fault if things don't succeed."

Manager types depend upon the vision and direction coming from above. They take the Dealers playbook and fully expect to succeed by supervising the organizations game strategy. They put that strategy out to their team in planning sessions and sales meetings and then rally the team around it.

➢ A Manager typically accomplish goals

Managers will organize and encourage the team, commit to a plan and work it to the letter. They know how to work hard and set goals, have regular meetings and offer bonuses and perks to keep the team motivated. Yet they never venture outside of the lines drawn by the Dealer. They may suggest, but will easily yield if those suggestions are questioned by the organization.

Because Managers concede to the authority and direction coming down from the organization they expect the team to do likewise in response to their Leadership. Those who run a tight desk want final sales floor decision making to come from them. The sales team must always bring each phase of a negotiation to the Manager for approval.

During this process, they will often beat a path back and forth, to and from the Managers desk in order to close a deal. They take the Customers next offer to the Manager and then return to the Customer with a counter offer or acceptance. This type of supervisor believes that the Salespersons success is a direct result of the sum of these back and forth interactions.

This hardball selling style does not fully empower the team and often requires the Manager to come in as the 'Closer' to make the final offer. The monthly unit sales goal is always in mind and each deal is based upon reaching that goal. I have known managers who will send a Salesperson home if they let a Customer leave before bringing the Manager in to put additional pressure on them, and that is not Leadership, that is management by fear.

Leaders, on the other hand, see the vision and develop a plan for accomplishing their goals. They build their team around the skills and abilities required to bring successful results and empower them to accomplish their own goals as a part of the whole.

➢ The Manager is well liked by upper management

As we have already seen, the Manager has many positive attributes, but often falls short in those that make for great Leadership. One of these positive characteristics is the ability to get along well with upper management. The Manager listens closely to his or her superiors and works hard to carry out the initiatives of the organization. This in turn brings the appreciation and respect of those in charge of the company.

Because Managers are liked by their superiors, they are usually comfortable in their positions. This can work for or against them depending upon how they perceive what must be done to achieve greater success and growing profits.

Most Managers recognize the need to encourage and support their staff, but they can be stern or condescending at times. Organization policies and goals dictate the Manager's behavior to those they lead.

When we review some of the characteristics of the Manager it is easy to see why they are liked by upper management. They are smart, trustworthy, respected, and usually have a history of success. They are loyal to the organization and good at accomplishing goals.

Managers who use their likeability to gain the confidence of the organization can have great leverage to innovate and to bring new and better ideas to the table.

➢ Managers can establish structure

This final attribute of the Manager character can be beneficial to both their current position and their ability to successfully make the transition to Leader. As Manager they know how to establish structure well, but they must avoid strict or confining methods that produce sales mimics rather than professionals who meet and exceed Customer expectations. Great Leadership depends heavily upon structure, but also recognizes the need for creative spontaneity and intuitive flexibility.

True Leadership is a fluid force, not a rigid set of rules and memorized idioms or catch phrases. While it is true that most buyers expect to be sold, today's consumers are more educated and prefer that the process be positive and relational. Customers typically feel threatened and disrespected when they are being pitched by a Salesperson.

Managers set the pace for their department and must model proper behavior by the way they view and treat both the Customer and the team. Their structure is clear and well defined, but it must not rule the day. It is a model not a final draft. To become an effective Leader you must break free from the strict confines of policy and security and take the courage to forge ahead to new ground.

A good Manager is a vessel into which Leadership can be poured. They are generally the highest level of contact for the Dealership therefore they represent the organization to the Customer. To make the jump from Manager to Leader, you must have confidence in your own ability to inspire and launch an initiative, coordinate and oversee its implementation, and bring it to a profitable conclusion. Do this and you will become indispensable to your organization.

Scenario

Tom had worked as a Salesperson in the local GM Dealership for over five years before becoming the Sales Manager there last year. He had always produced good numbers when he was selling, but was stumbling a bit as a Manager.

Travis is one of the Salespeople who works at the Dealership and has been there for nearly fifteen years. He was instrumental in helping Tom get started in sales, but never really aspired to be a Manager himself, he was just one of those guys that was happy selling cars.

One day, he and Tom were sitting in Tom's office talking about how things have been going since Tom became the new Sales Manager last year.

"Don't you think you should pay more attention to what the Salespeople are saying since they are the ones who hit the lot every day to talk with Customers?" Travis asked. *"You remember what that was like. Sometimes we had different ideas than what the folks upstairs wanted us to do, and sometimes ours worked better."*

Tom was busy preparing for tomorrows sales meeting, but he thought a moment before answering that question. *"That's not the way I do things Travis. I know the Salespeople think differently than the Managers, but let's face it, we all work for the Dealer and need to do it the way he tells us to.*

Travis chuckled a little about that, but he understood. *"Yes Tom, but he is a businessman and not a Salesman. He's a good man, but he doesn't really understand what makes a Salesman. Besides that, things are changing and he needs to recognize that and move the Dealership more into the direction the industry is going. It's all about Customer service and I can tell you this much: the*

Customer knows a lot more now than they used to and they expect us to treat them different because of it.

"Oh well" said Tom, giving a sign that he had said his piece.

Travis responded one more time with. *"You're the Manager. I'm just telling you how I feel about it and what some of the others are saying. With business going down you might want to listen to what they are saying. We have some very talented Salespeople on our staff and they have a lot of respect for what you did when you were selling. Still, they won't stay long if they aren't making enough money."*

"I promise to address it at the meeting tomorrow morning", said Tom.

The Morning Sales Meeting

"Of course we trust your judgment Tom, but let's face it; Customers don't like us having to get up from the table every five minutes to get numbers from the Manager. They feel like we are disrespecting them and don't have any real authority to accept their offer."

Angelo, one of the salespeople who worked at the Dealership and was usually a high producer, was trying to tell Tom about some ideas he had for selling from a different perspective. *"You remember that guy from last Friday. He just got up and walked out after you tried to come in and give him the hard close."*

"I've been talking to a friend who works at another Dealership" Angelo continued, *"and he says their Managers have been working with a Sales Leadership Coach learning how to do things differently. Sales there are up 20% in just two months."*

"Good for them" Tom replied, *"but that's them and you all know they have a new sales facility that looks pretty impressive. That's probably what's making the difference. Besides, the upper management here says they've been through this before. They're pretty sure it will all be back to normal again soon."* No one seemed too optimistic about that if you looked around the room at the faces on the Salespeople.

"Anyway, I understand. Just remember I'm only the Sales Manager and I have to do what the bosses tell me to do. You guys just need to go back to the basics and start taking more control of the deal. Customers are always griping about the prices. If it becomes an issue that just let me know and we'll match any deal they get elsewhere."

That comment seemed to bother Travis a little bit. He butted in, "*Hey Tom. We all respect you a lot, but people don't want to hear that anymore. They want to know why you just don't give them the best price right away. And when we do make that statement most never return*".

Tom replied with, "*You just bring the deals to me and I'll work the numbers. That's the way we've always done it here and I see no reason to change. Besides, the Dealer tells me he has a new ad that's running on the radio next week advertising 5% below invoice cost. That ought to bring them in for sure.*"

Later that day Anglo could be found at his friend's Dealership applying for a position in sales there. When they asked him why he was leaving the other Dealership he told them he really like working there, but he needed to make more money and if there was new training that was available at this Dealership he was ready to start right away.

They hired him on the spot and told him if any of the other Salespeople he knew from his old Dealership felt that way, they'd like to talk to them too.

What Tom, the Sales Manager, doesn't realize is that no matter how things worked in the past, if they aren't working now, as a Leader he needs to find out why and then find ways to effectively change them. But his loyalty is to the Dealer and the organization that has helped him so much and given him their trust as a Sales Manager. Unless they replace him, he plans to stay where he is and do what he has always done.

What is lacking in Tom as a Manager is Leadership. Once he achieves that goal upper management will view him in a different light. A manner that is in accordance with Leadership.

There are many Tom's out there who are in positions over their head and don't know how to get where they need to go. Without the proper training and knowledge they will usually end up fulfilling the role of Manager, but never becoming the real Leader that could make a big difference for themselves, the Dealership and for those who work under their supervision.

Tom still has respect in the Dealership, but it has now shifted from those who knew him as an exceptional Salesperson to those who have more to do with the administrative duties of the business. He has become a Manager type and his focus is much more on efficiency and structure, rather than on strong Leadership.

Leaders captain the ship, the ship does not captain them.

CHAPTER 7
CHARACTERISTICS OF A LEADER

Having spent many years in the automotive industry, I have met and worked with every type of Leader, from sales and service personnel to Dealership owners. During that time, I have seen the benefit of genuine Leadership and what happens in a Dealership where it is encouraged and active.

I write this book with an open eyed recognition of the many changes now occurring in the trade. Changes, which challenge the traditional views of both automotive industry professionals and the Customers they serve. While movies like 'Used Cars', 'Matilda' and more recently 'The Goods' have portrayed car people as low level hustlers, today's professionals paint a different picture. Some of the most qualified, educated and exceptional business Leaders in any industry are now found working in the automotive field.

Real professionals have abandoned the old "buyers are liars" mindset. They realize that in this highly competitive marketplace you have to earn someone's business. Today's Customers can expect to be treated with respect and integrity and no longer have to dread the car buying experience or compare it to a trip to the dentist.

➢ Characteristics of a Leader – Leaders are well liked

If you have read my book 'The Secrets of Inspirational Selling', you may remember the experience my wife and I had when buying her a new Mercedes. Though we had been through the typical sales experience at other Dealerships, we finally decided to look at a Mercedes. From the moment we arrived at the Mercedes Dealership every step of the process was a wonderful experience for us.

And what made it so different from what we had found elsewhere? The Salesperson! His highly professional approach to selling made the process extremely enjoyable and the decision to buy from him was very easy for both my wife and me.

In short, we liked him! He was a Leader in his field. The kind of professional our industry needs to overcome the negative stereotypes of the past and the challenges that are now facing those who choose a career in this business.

After purchasing the car, I was surprised to find out that he knew who I was and had recognized me from my work in the training industry. Yet it did not deter him in any way from giving us the full Customer experience that he used to sell vehicles to anyone who came to their Dealership. He did what he did because of who he was as a quality Salesperson, regardless of who I was as a Customer. That's what made him a Leader.

In these challenging economic times, we need Leaders at the helms of our Dealerships like never before. People like true Leaders. They emanate honesty, integrity, enthusiasm, commitment to self-improvement and genuine concern for others. Today's buyers demand quality from the people, products and service required to win their business. Such things will not come from slick hustlers with smooth tongues.

➢ Characteristics of a Leader – Respected

"R.E.S.P.E.C.T. Find out what it means to me." So goes the bridge to Aretha Franklin's great hit song that went to the top of the charts in 1967, and won her two Grammy Awards the following year.

But what does it really mean to be respected by others? The Dictionary defines respect in this way: "To consider worthy of esteem; to regard with honor." Neither esteem nor honor are given lightly. Especially in today's world where shady practices abound and have been highly expanded through the technology of the Internet.

Respect, much like the Grammy Award, is not easy to attain. It is given to those who excel in what they do and make a mark in life that causes others to esteem them worthy of honor. Great Leaders eventually get respect for what they do and how they do it. But it rarely comes easy and it never comes to those who sit on the sidelines and wait for life to happen.

In the business world, Leaders often must go against the tide to find the success that only comes to those who have the courage to seek it. At first glance, it may seem easy for some people to accomplish great things. *"If I had his talent I could make a difference too"*, some might say about a person who stands out above the crowd. Or of others, *"No wonder she's so successful. Look at the breaks she's had in her life."*

Take a deeper look and you will see that those who reach the pinnacle of success usually do so only after great dedication, hard work, and personal sacrifice. Like an Olympic athlete, it may look easy to wear the medal once it has been won, but the road that took them there was another story altogether. Leaders are willing to pay the price for success and they love nothing more than to share what they have learned with others who desire to achieve. For this, they are respected, and rightly so.

American Revolutionary writer, Thomas Paine once said, "Lead, follow or get out of the way." This is good advice for those who are seeking to achieve excellence in their life and career. To aspire to the heights that few achieve, you must reach for those things that few are willing to conceive. A Leader sees what needs to be done and gets to it when the time calls for action. Those who stand on the sidelines of life, can expect little more than whatever mediocrity affords.

Respect is earned and not given just because someone wants it. Take the time and be willing to make the necessary sacrifices that are required to succeed. You won't be sorry that you did. And, in the process, you may discover the answer to Aretha Franklin's great challenge to find out what *Respect* really means.

➢ Characteristics of a Leader – Admired

Admiration, like respect, comes to those who live in such a way as to demonstrate visible Leadership. Leadership is not turned on and off when it's needed. True Leaders live what they believe, because it has become a part of who they are.

Though some people are born with great potential for Leadership, that alone does not make them Leaders. Many born with exceptional abilities have ended up on the ash heap of life for their failure to use what gifts they have been given. Potential does not bring one admiration, only the development and proper use of it does.

Leaders carry themselves in such a way that their actions demand admiration. They don't seek it. It comes to them naturally as a result of their actions and interactions with others. They are admired by their peers and co-workers because they recognize and appreciate the value that others contribute. They give their best to those they lead, knowing that to do so is to cultivate success for all who truly desire it.

Someone once said, "The only things one can admire at length are those one admires without knowing why." But those who work with us and still admire us know why they do so. They have ample opportunity to see what we are really like, and there is nowhere to hide in the active environment of an automotive Dealership.

Leaders are admired because they launch out when others are still waiting for perfect weather. They weigh the risk against the reward and are willing to take their chances. Leaders don't sit around admiring themselves. They are too busy doing those things that awaken the admiration of others.

Look around you today and see who among your team members most desires to be led in what you have to offer. Their admiration for you can be used to create another future Leader.

➤ Characteristics of a Leader – People will follow them

Becoming a true Leader requires a willingness on your part to be responsible for those who will follow you. People follow Leaders because they want to be led. Sons want to be led by their fathers. If the father doesn't lead them they will eventually find someone else who will. It is human nature.

Never underestimate the powerful things one can learn from nature. Most species of animal life have a hierarchy that is organized around a Leader. As it is in the animal kingdom, so it is with men. Some are happy in life to just be grazers and as such need someone to guide them along the path of life. Leaders feel an inner sense that others need direction and they are willing to step up and do what is necessary for the benefit of the group.

When this happens a sense of security begins to develop and soon others are seeking to fulfill their own longing to become more than what they are. They begin to look for someone who can lead the way and thus, Leadership is born.

One of the difficult things a Leader must do to demonstrate their Leadership is to cull the herd of those who don't want to contribute. At first, this may seem harsh, but in so doing they clarify the objective and encourage others to do their best. Leaders who display the courage to make the hard choices will never lack loyal followers seeking to better themselves and advance toward their own goals for success.

Leaders draw others in their wake and help them reach their potential in the process. In so doing, the practice of managing people and tasks also further develops the Leader, and growth takes place in their abilities. The result of this growth often draws more people who are seeking strong Leadership in their career. True Leadership is infectious. It is a magnet for the hidden desires that all of us have to make a mark in life. It can unlock tremendous potential in anyone who will yield to its influence.

Everyone wants to be successful to some degree, but often they don't know what to do. A Leader will pursue the required knowledge and find the determination necessary to plow the road so others can come behind them. Like the trail Bosses of the early American migration West, Leaders bring a sense of order, security and confidence that causes others to believe in their vision and to follow them into the unknown.

Success does not come easily. Not everyone who sets off in search of it reaches their destination. But those who stay the course often reap great rewards. As you grow in your abilities to lead, those who truly desire to achieve will find their way to you. Don't take it personally when others move on to pastures where the grass is not as rich, but is easier to come by.

➢ Characteristics of a Leader – They know how to empower others

People who wish to succeed will follow a Leader who will show them the way. But not everyone desires the same level of success or will achieve the same as others do.

A great coach has on his or her team, athletes of every stature and of various levels of potential. Winning a Gold Medal is a tremendous achievement, but there is nothing shabby about the Silver or the Bronze.

A successful team has many different strengths and weaknesses. Their interdependence makes each member stronger and strengthens the team as a whole. Learn to see the unique qualities inherent in those you lead and strive to bring out the best that each has to offer. As a Leader you must help each of your employees discover the gifting within them and empower them to reach their peak potential. Education, encouragement, training, discipline, hard work and rewards are the tools of your trade.

The empowerment you provide will help your team members gain more control over their lives and develop more power for them to achieve success. But to empower someone is not just to give them permission to succeed. It is to provide the tools, training and guidance they need, and then to release them to do what needs to be done. Leaders help others catch their dreams, and in so doing, fulfill their own.

If employees are given the go-ahead to achieve, but the organization does not create an environment which fosters personal development, this is not empowerment.

As a Leader you must endeavor to gain the confidence of your superiors. With this you can accomplish great things and bring benefit to the whole organization. As others grow under your Leadership they force you upward in your own career.

Remember, great Leaders are always looking for other potential Leaders. They pass that attitude down to those under their direction, thus creating a chain of success that continues to grow and produce more Leaders.

A recent study by 'The Hay Group', an international organization that works with Leaders to transform business strategy into reality, confirmed that companies which focus on developing Leadership:

- Are nearly 40 percent more likely than peers to create the motivating climates which are proven to drive success

- Actively nurture Leadership behaviors and have a ready pool of successors for critical roles

Your commitment to develop great Leadership will empower those you lead, and release further empowerment from those who have chosen you to be a Leader in their organization. This can only enhance the potential for growth in those you lead as well as in your own career, and in the Dealership organization as a whole.

Scenario

Mythical Motors was a family owned Dealership that had been operating for over 45 years in their city. The founder had two sons who ran the sales departments at the Dealership. Robert, the elder son, was the New Car Manager and James was in charge of the Used Car Department. Their father still worked as the GM as he had always done since founding the business.

Being a well established Dealership there was plenty of business to go around so the two brothers worked quite well together with very little friction. Each of them had eight Salespeople in their department that were assigned to them by their father.

Although Mythical Motors was surviving, the economy was presenting real challenges and made the father concerned that they might need to rethink how they ran their Dealership. There were a lot of new ideas floating around and he thought it would be good to see if they might have some value for helping them develop new business.

The three of them had decided to send James to a Leadership Training Seminar taking place in a nearby city, and James returned to the Dealership with a lot of new ideas he wanted to implement in the sales departments. He felt that the changes taking place in the retail automotive industry merited looking at some new methods that might help them grow. He shared some of the ideas with his brother Robert, but he did not like the ideas stating that the only thing that needed changing was the economy and when that occurred business would go back to normal.

The father, being a wise businessman, decided to let James implement the changes in his department, while Robert continued doing business as he always had. The brothers agreed to this and James was soon training his employees with an emphasis on Team Building as a Leader, rather than running the department as a Boss with family authority. The one thing they continued was the tradition of having their weekly sales meetings together with all the sales team members present from both departments.

At first, things slowed down a bit in used cars sales because James was spending a lot of time individually with his Salespeople implementing what he had learned at the Seminar. He tried his best to encourage them that once they became a real team they would see their sales increase and, although they were a bit concerned that they were spending their time training rather then walking the lot like they usually did, they all said there was a definite difference in the environment of their department as they were not so much competing with each others as they had before.

In the New Car Department things were running as usual and Robert, who was a real Boss type of supervisor, kept a tight reign on things and made sure no one let a Customer off the lot before bringing them to him for a final shot at closing. In his mind if you were a real Salesperson you could make a deal work and if you couldn't he wanted to know why. He worked every deal tightly and there wasn't much room for error.

It wasn't long though before sales began to rise in the Used Car Department and the weekly meetings became quite different. Robert would make sure his team went out knowing what needed to be done and the mistakes they had each made that week. James on the other hand spent much of his time encouraging his team for their hard work and the positive changes he could see in how the Customers were reacting to what the Salespeople were doing. Even though they were selling a few less used cars at first, their profits were increasing as they focused on listening to what the Customers wanted and less on just selling them a car and getting them out the door.

Within a few months there was a clear difference in how things worked in the two departments and it wasn't long before many of the Salespeople working for Robert asked if they could move over to the Used Car Department. They liked what some of James' Salespeople there were telling them and thought it could help them do more business if they learned some of the new things he was teaching his team. The only way they could switch though was if someone from used cars would swap places and no one there was willing to make that change.

Their father, being a wise business man, spent much of his time speaking to Customers from both departments and the ones who bought used cars seemed to be extremely happy about their purchase and their buying experience. Even the Service Department Manager commented on how the used car team was helping his business by bringing their Customers through a Service Walk and introducing them to him and his service team as part of the sales process.

Those who purchased new cars seemed to be the same as always and saw their purchase as a matter of what they had to do rather than an enjoyable experience. The buyer surveys they sent out showed a marked difference in Customer satisfaction between the two departments as well.

Before long, business was growing and profits increased largely because of what was happening in the Used Car Department. Even Robert had to admit that what James had learned at the Leadership Seminar obviously was making a difference and he asked his brother to take over both departments for a week while he attended the same training for himself.

After a year had passed Mythical Motors was doing so well they decided to open another Dealership in a nearby town and Robert went off to become the new GM while James took over the entire Sales Department at their original Dealership. Their father felt certain now that he could retire soon and that the company he had built would be in good hands with both of his sons being real Leaders in the business.

Though Mythical Motors is just that, in reality these types of changes are taking place in many Dealerships where Leadership is being taught and Dealers and Managers are seeing the great benefits of learning true team development focused on meeting and exceeding the Customers wants and needs.

The processes and ideas found in this book can help any Dealership that wants to increase their business and their Customer base, that is, if they will implement what is found here. I know this to be true because after more than twenty-five years of teaching these principles I have seen what true Leadership can bring to a Dealership.

Are you ready for to be that true Leader?

CHAPTER 8 FOUR THOUGHTS ABOUT LEADERSHIP

As we have already seen, Leadership is essentially about character. It can be learned, but to be sustained and natural it is dependent upon certain inherent traits of human character. Things like selfishness, isolationism, laziness, procrastination, extreme arrogance; characteristics such as these negate a person's potential for effective Leadership. One must tackle these before attempting to become a successful Leader.

I use the word *sustained* because the nature of Leadership is progressive. It gets better as it is being practiced. Because of its interactive nature it requires participation with others; hence Leaders cannot function without followers. But even more important, Leadership must be earned from those who choose to follow. Forced Leadership is not necessarily true Leadership, but rather a form of Command, as in military rank.

In my experience, there are four essential aspects of Leadership that must be considered for those who desire to become effective in their positions as Leaders.

1. You have to earn the status of Leader

True Leadership must be earned. Others aren't going to see you as their Leader just because you want them to. You will have to earn your Leadership status the hard way. You will have to prove to those around you that you are indeed a Leader.

If you are a Manager at your Dealership, that doesn't mean you take out the company organizational chart and point out to your subordinates that your position on the chart is higher up than theirs, thus making you their Leader. Nor will reading this book automatically guarantee your status as a Leader to those you supervise. I will give you the necessary tools and guidance, but Leadership development is done on the job. It produces its best fruit in the garden of experience.

Leadership status is earned by what you do everyday working with those around you. As you implement the actions and attitudes I will show you, and teach others to do the same, you will not only become a successful Leader, you will cultivate an environment of success throughout your Dealership.

As former President John F. Kennedy once said, "*A rising tide lifts all boats.*" People follow Leaders because their actions produce positive results that affect everyone involved. When efficiency, profits and growth take place under your supervision you will not have to remind others that you are the Leader. They will follow you gladly because of the positive effect your Leadership is having on their own life and career.

Terms like, '*Whatever you say, you're the Boss*' will soon be replaced with phrases like, '*That's a great idea. I'm with you all the way.*' Both of these statements imply a commitment, and an affirmation of your Leadership.

Proof of Leadership is not displayed by the way you talk, dress or give commands. It is seen through the growth and quality of those you lead and the resulting changes that take place in your work environment. The idea of dressing for success certainly has some value for professional appearance, but no matter how much you spend on your next suit of clothes, wearing them will not make you a Leader. It's the person in the suit that makes a difference, not the suit they are wearing.

Begin to envision yourself as a successful Leader and practice those things that great Leaders do every day. As you continue in this book you will see more of the qualities that you must develop in order to become a strong Leader. As you do this you will earn the respect and support of those you work with.

2. Once you reach the level of Leader, you still have the characteristics of a Boss and Manager within you

In many ways, Leaders are Bosses and Managers who have continued to grow in their knowledge and abilities, and aspire to reach greater heights in their life and career. All of us at some point find ourselves in the comfort zone. It is what we do with that time that makes the difference. Leaders see that happening, shake the dust of their feet and get back to the process of growth and change.

Many of the characteristics of the Boss or Manager types are good qualities to have, and when properly implemented, they can be a launch pad for great Leadership. If you have discovered in yourself some of the attributes of either a Boss or Manager as I presented them to you, please don't be offended. My purpose was not to demean Bosses or Managers in any way. As I mentioned in previous chapters they are smart, hard working, diligent, trustworthy, loyal, and able to accomplish. But they are part of the *'old way'* that must be outgrown in order for transformation to take place in our industry.

Those of us who are determined to see that happen recognize how crucial it is that we make an honest assessment of where we are and how we got here. Only then can we go forward with confidence. Like the GPS unit in your car, unless you have a starting point to go by, you cannot get proper directions to where you are headed. In other words, knowing just where you are right now is essential before mapping out the right path that will take you to your desired destination.

Never underestimate the value of knowing who and where you are. Learning how to transform the qualities that got you where you are now into those that will take you where you want to go can be an important key to your success as a Leader.

Creating your roadmap to successful Leadership is no different. The more you understand where you are and how you got here, the better chance you have of getting where you want to go. Let's face it, if Leadership was so easy, everyone would be doing it. There are more Bosses and Managers currently working in our Dealerships because Leadership requires a commitment to change that many are not willing to make.

Once you have decided in yourself to make that change, it is important to remember that Leadership is sustained by the continuous practice of the right principles, and by an unwavering commitment to further growth and development.

Moving from the old to the new requires Leaders who will step up and take the challenges that come with being in the forefront of change. Like the heat shield on the Space Shuttle, these characteristics must remain firmly in place in order to protect your position as Leader among those you supervise.

3. If you change jobs you start again as a Boss and have to re-earn the level of Leader

It is very important to remember that Leadership is relational. You can only lead those who will allow you the privilege, and you must first earn their trust before that will happen. Because it is based upon a relationship of trust, confidence and respect, Leadership must be re-earned if you change jobs and have new people who call you Boss.

Proper team building is not just getting a group of people to agree on a certain method or approach to doing business. It is relational in nature and there is a sort of chemistry that happens within a group when those involved are learning to function as an effective team.

The interaction and inter-dependency that develops during team building is the glue that holds it together and allows for proper Leadership to be expressed.

A functioning team is like a well oiled machine in which each part depends upon every other part to perform at its highest level of efficiency. It matters not whether it's a sales team, a musical ensemble, or a team of horses; effective teamwork always produces results.

Some Leaders have been known to turn down a better paying job offer if it meant leaving a team they have successfully built. On the other hand, some employees will follow a Leader wherever they go rather than give up what they have working together. That certainly happens a lot in the retail automotive business.

An effective Dealership team is a lot like a family. No one wants to break up a family that's doing great together and demonstrating excellence. You probably have known a Department Manager who left for greener pastures elsewhere, only to find themselves coming up short when compared to what they were producing at their former Dealership. When that happens, a Leader quickly realizes the value that his or her previous co-workers added to the success and effectiveness of their Leadership.

That doesn't mean that you shouldn't take advantage of a promotion or a better job if the opportunity comes available. It just means you should be aware of the fact that in your new position you will start over again as a Boss. Sometimes change is unavoidable and is a natural part of progressing upward on your career path.

When you have properly developed the Leadership qualities you will learn from this book, you will take them with you wherever you go. They will become building blocks for your next venture of success. Every step on your career path is another opportunity for growth and learning. You don't have to burn the bridges you leave behind you when you are a truly effective Leader. Instead, they form a trail that is a testament to how you got to where you are now. Even this can play an essential part in your ability to affect change and growth, and for earning the respect of those you supervise in your new position or dealership.

4. You have to indirectly get people's permission to lead them

No matter what others may think about car Salespeople, the self confidence that it takes to get up every day and go out on a sales floor and produce is not common to everyone. If you have been a supervisor for any length of time you have likely discovered that most people, especially those in sales, think they know how best to do their job.

You may have someone under your supervision who regularly produces great numbers every month. You could learn a lot from them. Just ask them and they will tell you if they haven't already. Whether it is ego driven or not, let's face it, when you need their numbers you are glad they are there.

Because of this, a Manager will often overlook some of their quirky or questionable methods in favor of the results they get. This can make it difficult to establish your authority if you compromise Leadership principles in favor of team members who depend only upon their numbers to give them favor. Taking an existing team and getting their permission to lead them in a new direction or with a new approach can present a big challenge. Some team members may even call you to account if you allow a superstar mentality to dominate how you lead or don't lead high producers.

Leadership requires legitimacy and validation. Legitimacy comes from your appointment to lead by the organization. Validation must come from those you lead. For example: You have a monthly sales goal that you would like to reach and you put that out to the team in your Monday morning meeting.

- *The Boss says, "Here's what we're going to do this month. I expect everyone to do their part."*

- *The Manager says, "Here's how we've done it before. Just do what we did and it will work again."*

- *The Leader says, "I have some ideas on how to accomplish this and I'd like to go over them with each of you to get your input."*

As a Leader you have just indirectly asked for their permission to lead them and suggested that you view their ideas as valuable.

How you talk to team members about other team members – including those in upper management – can also be an effective way to indirectly gain permission to lead. If your conversation is positive you have indirectly encouraged trust among your team members. If it is negative you subvert your Leadership and render it ineffective in the eyes of those you lead.

When you, as the Leader, speak positively about those who work with you, you encourage an environment that is supportive and validating for them as well as for yourself. Often, it is the little things that make the difference in whether or not your team members will entrust you with the privilege to lead them; gaining permission to do so from those on your team is an essential element to your success as a Leader.

CHAPTER 9
QUALITIES OF A STRONG LEADER

Author Steven Covey's 1990 bestseller, '7 Habits of Highly Effective People', clearly demonstrated that there are common practices all great Leaders follow in their daily life.

His groundbreaking study of successful Leadership revealed a consistent pattern of routines and thought patterns common to people of great achievement.

As we delve into the qualities that make someone an exceptional Leader you will see that strong Leadership does not happen by chance. It is the result of consistent and repetitive actions and disciplined thought processes. Leaders take the initiative and are motivated by the belief that consistent growth, decisive action and effective decision making are the determining factors for success in life.

Strong Leaders are confident in what they do, and their ability to impart these qualities to their followers is proof that success is available for all who will consistently practice certain routines proven to produce success.

➢ Qualities of a Strong Leader – I don't have to remind people that work for me that I am a strong Leader

Someone once said, "The only problem with winning the Humility Award is that you can't display it anywhere for others to see." As I stated in a previous chapter a Leader doesn't actively seek personal recognition. They are too busy being Leaders to do that. Their recognition comes naturally as a result of their achievements.

Those in Leadership positions, who constantly have to remind others that they are in control, have yet to shed some of the negative aspects of the 'Boss' supervisor type. As a strong Leader, you must possess the assurance to manage others without the need of constant personal affirmation. Your confidence must be in the process and philosophy which you employ, and the growing progress of those you lead.

When you constantly remind others of your own authority and value, you betray a lack of self confidence.

This will eventually be seen by them as a weakness and will affect your ability to lead them successfully. As a successful Leader, your results will speak for you. If you are confident that what you are doing will produce the desired results, you don't need to apologize or question whether your team knows who is in control.

What is critical to strong Leadership though is that your goals have genuine value and are worthy of attaining. This will allow you to be free to focus on your team and the goals they have set for themselves and for the group as a whole. If your goals and guidance are clear to those you lead and are producing results, your Leadership will not need to be constantly restated.

Sometimes when Leadership is functioning at its best, it may seem like your workers are doing their own thing independent of you. If things are going well without them running back and forth to the Managers desk, be thankful for that. Your team is doing what you have taught them do.

In your interactions with team members, make sure they are clear on what you expect of them. If you find yourself constantly having to restate your authority, it may be time to sit down with them and revisit the goals and objectives that you desire to accomplish together.

Remember, strong Leadership does not require a heavy handed management style. As you grow in your role, you will find it to be a natural force flowing from the confidence that comes from your commitment to quality.

➢ Qualities of a Strong Leader – I view each person who I lead as an individual

As a Leader, part of my job is to take the resources I have available to me – including the human resources – and utilize them to accomplish the goals and objectives I have set for David Lewis & Associates. As the President and Leader of my own company, I operate on the same principles that I teach to Leaders like you. I have a team of people, a specific set of resources, and I have my own set of goals and objectives.

Each person who works for me is an individual with specifics talents, needs and desires. Their life exists both inside and outside of the workplace. If I forget that, I might make the mistake of treating them more like a commodity than a person. In order to successfully lead my team I must get to know them. I must respect each of them for whom they are, and do my best to understand their talents, dreams and goals.

Our lives intersect both at and away from the workplace. This is important for both them and me if we are to accomplish the goals that each of us have in order to have a full and rich life. If they are struggling with personal issues, an illness in the family or financial problems, I want to know this. There may be something I can do to help them.

This is both for their benefit and to protect their ability to function well in the workplace. The more I know about the people I lead, the better I can lead them.

Every person is different and each one will respond differently to my Leadership. If I don't know this I cannot properly assess the best way to guide those I lead to the success they desire. Getting to know the nature and personality of those I lead can only enhance my ability to nurture them successfully.

A team is like a family. You must get to know each one individually; to find out what makes them tick. As a strong Leader, your knowledge and support of each individual team member is vital for creating a workplace environment that cultivates both individual and group success.

➢ Qualities of a Strong Leader – Most days I look forward to going to work

As a Strong Leader, I must constantly view what I do as an opportunity to implement the things I am learning, and to teach others. As long as I keep exposing myself to new ideas and philosophies I will always look forward to going to work.

It is important to set long term, short term, and daily goals. My daily goals give me a clear work plan and, when accomplished, give me the satisfaction of a day well spent. My short and long term goals keep me motivated to come in the next day knowing that I still have something that I want and need to accomplish.

As a Leader, it is important to instruct your team in the proper use and purpose of goal setting. When everyone has a clear idea of what they are to accomplish they can always look forward to coming to work.

Never go to work without knowing what you want to achieve that day. Yet be prepared also to deal with things that require spontaneous action. You must plan your day complete with interruptions.

Where there is no vision, disorder and complacency take over. Without clear goals your work will become a wandering generality with little or no satisfaction or accomplishment. Discontentment in the workplace can sap team energy and reduce production. As a Leader you must set the pace by bringing new and exciting ideas to the table and having a clear plan for their implementation.

When people love what they are doing they look forward to doing it again. This is the same for you as a Leader as it is for those you lead. The enthusiasm you bring to the Dealership each day will spill over onto those around you, from your staff, to the management and also to the Customers.

As a Leader, everything you do is an example for those you lead. You must make the atmosphere you work in inviting, fun and exciting. When you do, both you and your team will find yourselves coming in early and leaving late. Great Leadership provides clear objectives with a viable plan and obtainable rewards. When these are in place, workplace malaise is rare.

➢ Qualities of a Strong Leader – I recognize the position I hold as an opportunity to learn

True Leaders never stop learning. Their position not only requires that they do so to be successful, but often affords them access to those things that will further develop their skills and knowledge. Leaders who cease to learn cease to lead.

As a Leader, you hold the key to how far your team will go in educating themselves for their job. Whether it is product knowledge, inspirational selling techniques, Customer service or goals and planning, you must lead the way for your team. If your team members perceive they know more than you do, or are more motivated to learn than you, they may lose their incentive to follow your Leadership.

An Automobile Dealership is not a stagnant environment where the teacher uses a book of fixed knowledge on a given topic. Anything can happen on any given day. You must be flexible and prepared at the same time. There are many different sources of available information and training that present innovative techniques for helping your team achieve success. All offer some value that can be added to your Leadership tool chest. Because of the variety of personalities, abilities and experience of those you lead, the more equipped you are with available knowledge and training, the better your chance of success as a Leader.

Avoid the comfort zone when it comes to knowledge and learning. Involve yourself and your team in industry activities and training opportunities that will motivate them to reach high levels of achievement. Authentic Leadership requires a commitment to learning and advancing the skills for success. Use your position as a springboard to reach higher and take others with you as you rise.

➢ Qualities of a Strong Leader – The people I lead are willing to work beyond their job description

Strong Leaders know the value of their team. They step aside when credit is given and allow their team members to shine. They are self confident and let their teams results speak for them instead. When this happens, their workers feel the pride of personal accomplishment and they will constantly strive to meet and exceed their Leader's expectations.

Effective Leaders know that giving affirmation for a job well done is a performance booster for those who receive it. Because of this, they consistently receive over the top performance from the people they lead. Have you ever managed someone who required daily intervention to produce barely acceptable results? People who are not appreciated are not motivated to strive for excellence. Learning how to motivate co-workers is an essential skill a strong Leader must possess in today's ever-changing workplace.

Researchers at the University of Nebraska–Lincoln examined sources of motivation of Nebraska workers in urban and rural settings. The results have demonstrated that five unique sources of motivation exist. Those primary motivators are:

- Fun
- Rewards
- Reputation
- Challenge
- Cause or Purpose

When you understand what drives individual workers, you can create an environment and structure that not only encourages performance, but constantly raises the level of it among those you lead. Your success as a strong Leader is never more visible than when it is seen through the dedication, personal growth, and quality of performance of those you lead.

➤ Qualities of a Strong Leader – My primary objective is to assist others in reaching their goal

People willingly go above and beyond in their job performance when they work for a strong Leader. They are committed to the Leaders objectives because they recognize that same commitment in their Leader toward them. A strong Leader is always focused on the goals that they have set for themselves, but their method of reaching them is through helping others reach their goals.

Like an orchestra conductor, the strong Leader guides and encourages each player to work together in harmony to make the full composition effective. Strong Leaders direct the process of attaining their goals as a conductor expresses Leadership through the individual musicians playing their parts. They set the tempo and hold the players together by direction and correction given from their central position as Leader.

In a finely tuned staff, each person has his or her eye on the tasks at hand, which are coordinated by the Leaders guidance and direction. He or she sets the pace and keeps the team focused on the target each has for their own success.

Strong Leaders only realize their own success through the combined results of those they have trained and directed. Each team member has unique gifts and abilities which must be blended and coordinated to accomplish the desired outcome.

In your role as Leader, you cannot help others achieve their objectives unless you know clearly what they are shooting for. Get to know the specific goals of each team member and their daily plans on how to accomplish them. Goals must be realistic and achievable and suited to the unique abilities of each person. Like the conductor who is tuned in to any sharp or flat notes coming from his orchestra, learn to spot areas where tuning up needs to take place.

Goals must also be challenging in order to stretch and grow those you are leading. As you increase your own capacity to reach higher, those you lead will rise with you in their skills and performance.

Strong Leadership in action is much like a great musical composition. It has its highs and lows, moments of serenity, powerful crescendos, repetitive choruses and inspiring solo performances, all artfully directed toward a powerful finale.

Also in retail auto sales, each step of the process provides an additional comfort to the Customer and takes them through several steps filled with information, excitement, and positive stimulation; all leading to the eventual finale of a successful sale. Leaders who train their sales staff to perform in this way will experience a growing Customer base, increasing profits, and a satisfied sales team regularly reaching and exceeding their sales goals.

➢ Qualities of a Strong Leader – Most find it easy and enjoyable to work for me

Can you think of a job you once had, or a particular period in your career, when you didn't enjoy your work because of someone you worked for? What could be more miserable than going to work every day and hating the fact that you are there? Yet most people list their Boss as the person with whom they have the least pleasant interactions at work. Strong Leaders know how important it is that employees enjoy their work. They also know that their own Leadership and Management style plays a crucial part in that equation.

With the cost of training new employee's skyrocketing, excessive turnover can certainly rob productivity and profits. Knowing how to retain staff is a vital part of a successful Leaders skill set. Your efforts to provide a solid career path for your staff and to promote a work/ life balance for them will encourage stability in both their personal life and their profession.

Listen to your employees and give constructive criticism when necessary, always balanced with recognition and appreciation for the work they do well. Always keep your word and expect the same from your staff. The value of honesty and integrity in a Dealership cannot be overstated when it comes to employee contentment. Leaders who invest sufficient time and effort in the development of their staff create a bond that breeds loyalty, productivity and a happy work environment.

As a Leader, you must see your employees as unique individuals and be clear about what you expect of them on a daily basis. Know their strengths and weaknesses, and celebrate their successes with them when they do well. No matter how much you value your position, unless your Leadership cultivates happy and productive employees your job security and success is always at risk.

True Leadership is not measured by how happy you are as a Leader. It is measured by the happiness, productivity and success of those you lead.

➢ Qualities of a Strong Leader – I know my strengths and weaknesses

Thus far, much of what I have said about Leadership dealt with the way Leaders view and act toward those whom they supervise. These are important aspects of strong Leadership for sure and never to be ignored or taken lightly. How a Leader views themselves is just as important. The level of openness that strong Leaders have with themselves is critical for the development of how they will fulfill their Leadership role.

One of the great things about knowing yourself is learning just how much you need other people. Knowing your own weaknesses is the beginning of real strength. Often weaknesses are really potential strengths that have yet to be developed. Strong Leaders are not afraid to view their own weaknesses. They use that knowledge to identify what strengths others can provide more effectively in accomplishing the team goals.

If you ever tried to row a boat with one arm you would soon find yourself going in circles and quickly recognize the value of another arm; especially if you found yourself headed into troubled waters. Even so, Leaders who fail to recognize their own weaknesses may find themselves going in circles unable to accomplish much.

Often, the ability to go straight ahead towards victory depends upon the balance that others bring to our effort. Strong Leaders value the camaraderie of team effort. Their staff becomes an extension of themselves and enhances their ability to reach the desired objective.

Former President Dwight D. Eisenhower once said, "Only strength can cooperate. Weakness can only beg." When we properly understand our own weaknesses we can better assess our strengths and learn how to utilize them effectively. Often it is our interactions with others that allow us to observe our own selves with more clarity.

Leaders who don't know their strengths and weaknesses cannot properly manage and utilize the talents of those they lead. When duties need to be designated to staff members, it is critical to know who can best accomplish the required actions. If you as Leader fail to properly evaluate these things you may overburden yourself with tasks that could be accomplished by others. When this happens it can frustrate the process as well as yourself and the people you lead.

Strong Leadership is a balance of give and take. You must see your team members as those who come alongside you and enhance your strengths as well as compensate for your weaknesses.

➢ Qualities of a Strong Leader – I genuinely like most people

People who don't like others can never become strong Leaders, and will at best, be terrible Bosses. Because of that I never recommend this business to people who don't like people. The daily interaction with other employees as well as Customers and upper management would be an exercise in futility.

As Barbra Streisand once so beautifully put it, *"People who love people are the luckiest people in the world."* They are lucky because they experience life with all of the potentials that others bring into it. The loner has no familiarity with such things.

Working together with others to accomplish goals and objectives can be both challenging and exhilarating. Those who don't like others, have no one with which to share either their moments of trial, or those of victory. Strong Leaders genuinely like others and care about their well being. They recognize the value they bring to others as well as what they receive in return. It is an essential ingredient of true Leadership.

Selfishness and Leadership are mutually exclusive. Like oil and water they can never truly blend, because they have no complimenting attributes. Employees and subordinates are more likely to follow a Leader who puts the needs of the team above their own interests first. Those who are perceived to be in it for themselves rarely enjoy the support of their team members.

Again, we see that Leadership and relationship are undeniably linked. You cannot genuinely like someone with whom you have no relationship. Neither can you have a trusting relationship with someone you don't like.

From the patron's perspective, Managers who don't like people often deal with Customers in such a way as to reinforce the old idea that car dealers are all crooks and just out to get them. I've seen many people walk out on a purchase just because they felt the one in charge did not have their best interest in mind. Certainly it is the death of repeat business. And we've all known good staff people who left their jobs because they found no way to please the Manager or because he or she just didn't like them.

Get to know those who you lead and make a genuine effort to show an interest in them as people, as well as in their career. Leaders who do this find their own lives to benefit greatly from it as well. Leadership and business are best accomplished at a table where friends sit together.

➤ Qualities of a Strong Leader – I continually reach my goal

As we have clearly seen, strong Leaders recognize the necessity of healthy relationships and the interdependence required to accomplish team goals and objectives.

Successful Leaders continually reach their goals because they lead a team that effectively utilizes what they have been taught in order to accomplish their own individual goals. The influence that Leadership affords can only be sustained if Leaders continually reach their own objectives. Failure to do so, can drain employee motivation and greatly inhibit productive behavior.

Strong Leaders realize the close interconnection between their staff's individual goals and the goals they have set for themselves. If these things are not in harmony, you cannot reach a successful conclusion. To avoid this, Leaders constantly assess the goals of the team as well as their own, and that of the Dealership. Long term objectives can only be met if daily and short term goals are being achieved.

You may remember the Manager that I used to work for which I referred to in an earlier chapter. He always to set the monthly goals based on selling eighty cars a month. He never raised the bar, but often lowered it during months that were notoriously slow in previous years. His Leadership was uninspiring and left much to be desired.

Don't be afraid to set goals for your team that have not been achieved before. But make sure you are not using the same old strategies trying to accomplish the new goals. Stating exaggerated goals to raise excitement in a meeting has no value without planning and implementing new strategies for their accomplishment.

Long term goals are reachable only if they are effectively broken into sizeable pieces and distributed properly according to individual team abilities. Strong Leaders know that daily goals are action oriented and must not require the input of others to be accomplished. Regular contacts with previous Customers or follow-up to recent ones, are examples of this type of daily action.

Dealership goals are not to be discussed with sales team members, only goals that are to be individually accomplished or are to be the result of the combined effort of the team. As an effective Leader you must monitor and oversee team goal reaching activities. You must also have daily goals that are for yourself and independent of their actions.

Leadership success is the result of a multitude of factors and individual efforts brought together to accomplish something that cannot normally be done without the cooperation of others.

➢ Qualities of a Strong Leader – Good people want to work for me

Working with good people can make Leadership a wonderful experience for everyone involved. The measure of great Leaders is often confirmed by those who want to work for them. Strong Leaders carry themselves in such a way that others are naturally drawn to them. In some cases, strong Leaders seem to be able to accomplish great things almost effortlessly.

We often hear the term *work smart* used in contrast to the idea of *work hard.* Working smart is in fact often the matured fruit of a solid work hard ethic. Though some Leaders may seem to float on a sea of God given talent, they almost always arise from a commitment to dedication, hard work and self determination. Someone once said, "You can't lead effectively until you have learned to serve others." I don't know if that's an absolute truth, but it certainly sounds like a good one.

In our modern world, we have largely forsaken the idea of apprenticeship programs. What a shame! It seems like many these days want to shoot straight to the top with as little sweat as possible along the way. On the other hand, Leaders are generally molded in the furnace of experience. They know how to lead because they learned it from someone else, and often several someone else's. Because of this, others who are seeking to better their own selves and accomplish great things, desire to work for them.

Good people always look for quality Leaders to which they can join themselves. In the same way, strong Leaders have a high regard for those who desire to learn from them. They approach Leadership seriously so as not to disrespect the dedication and honor given to them by their employees.

Developing the type of Leadership that others want to follow is an art form not just a job. It is something that demands a respect for self and others, as well as for the career you have chosen.

Strong Leaders often view their employees as partners that carry out the implementation of those things over which they administrate. They don't feel a necessity to establish strict lines of authority because they are already understood by both parties. Successful Leadership requires a delicate balance of authority, training, personal relationship and effective interaction. When these are present in a Leader, others feel compelled to follow them.

➢ Qualities of a Strong Leader – I am constantly setting and reaching higher goals for myself

Great Leaders constantly aspire to reach beyond what they have already achieved. Not just because it is there, but for the value that doing so brings to their lives and to those around them. Doing something to the best of one's abilities is a central principle for higher achievement to Leaders. As they increase their knowledge and training, the natural result is a desire to reach higher and produce more.

Because Strong Leaders are visionaries, they are drawn on by the challenge of what lies ahead. They don't aim randomly at a big picture. They know there are specific and ordered steps to be taken if they are to succeed over the sometimes long course of accomplishing their objectives. They must first have a *clear picture* of what they desire to achieve, followed by a *step by step plan* of how to bring it to completion.

Next, they *inspire others to participate* and to bring their talents and abilities to bear on achieving the objective. They then lay out *clear directions and specific goals* that must be met in order to succeed.

Once they are satisfied that their plan will work and that they have the necessary resources in place, they begin to *execute the planned process* to bring about a successful conclusion. They then step up and *manage the process* and direct and coordinate those assigned to individual tasks in order to accomplish the final outcome they desire.

In some sense, everything in a business stands or falls on the visions and actions of Leadership. Strong Leaders are willing to step up and do what needs to be done to take things forward when necessary.

Renowned playwright George Bernard Shaw spoke about the way of visionary Leadership saying, "You see things; and you say, 'Why?' But I dream things that never were; and I say, "Why not?"

Being a Strong Leader in our industry is not for the timid, or for those who look for a simple life. The complexities of the auto business are many, but opportunity abounds. If you are willing to dream big and immerse yourself in the knowledge and skill development that is required for successful Leadership the prospects are almost limitless.

What industry can compare to the business we are in? Our modern world was built by those who dared to reach for higher ground and were not satisfied with the status quo. Just so, strong Leadership requires those willing to stretch themselves and to encourage those around them to keep reaching when others say. . . *Enough!*

➢ Qualities of a Strong Leader – I give my best in whatever I do

Strong Leaders never knowingly commit to something that is menial or worthless. But when they do commit to a task they follow it through to the end and give it all they have. To them, anything worth doing is worth doing well. Much like the 'Good Housekeeping Seal of Approval', a true Leader believes that a reputation for quality and integrity in their work is worth any sacrifice.

In the old days, a Car Sales Manager could go from city to city without having to worry about their reputation following them. If they could convince the Dealer that they could do the job, they usually got hired. Today, we live in a transparent world where what we did this morning can be shouted from the housetops by nightfall. It is scary indeed, but at the same it invokes a return to quality and integrity.

If you are not willing to do your best at what you do you will likely have to settle for less than someone who will.

It's harder now to *get away with it* than it used to be. And why shouldn't it be? People who hire you, work for you or spend their money to purchase your product or service deserve the best effort and quality you have to give.

To quote Oprah Winfrey, "Doing the best at this moment puts you in the best place for the next moment." And for a strong Leader that statement rings true.

Leaders know the value of putting first things first and prioritizing their work so as to attain top efficiency and productivity. They take the opportunity when it is there and never put off for later the things that can be done now.

There's something magic about doing the best you can. It causes others around you to want to do the same. Like marathon runners, when one has run his leg of the race another picks up the baton and goes on. From there anything can happen.

Leadership is not about the size of your vision or goal, it is about the value that you place on what you do and the commitment that you have to doing it well. Being a part of something larger than just you is empowering and can release qualities that only come from joining with others to accomplish the extraordinary.

➢ Qualities of a Strong Leader – I am a problem solver

Hopefully, as we have examined the qualities of strong Leaders you have begun to apply some of these principles to your own life and management style. As a Leader you must learn to be proactive when it comes to dealing with the many problems that can arise in your Dealership. Great Leaders see problems as opportunities.

Whether it is trouble with a Customer, a team member, or is product or service related, if it is in your department, take the responsibility to deal with it as soon as it occurs. Effective problem solving separates those who become strong Leaders from those who are not willing to take the front line in times of crisis.

In the automobile industry, we have seen many changes being implemented recently to meet the demands that Customers have today for quality of products and service. Take the used car business as an example. Used cars are now marketed as *Pre-Owned* and can be covered with extended warranties.

How did this come about? Somewhere an innovative Leader saw that by removing the fear factor often attached to buying a used vehicle, Customers would flock to the opportunity to save money; especially if they could have an assurance of quality and reliability.

Soon, one manufacturer came up with the term 'Certified Pre-Owned Vehicle' and the reputation for quality that accompanied that brand was now assigned to used vehicles that were traded in and resold from their lots. Next, the manufacturers offered factory warranties to vehicles that their Dealerships would inspect and repair before being resold.

All of this happened because a strong Leader in each situation saw the problems, found a solution, and took the necessary actions to turn them into opportunities. The 'Certified Pre-Owned' car business is booming right now as new car prices rise, the economy struggles, and credit becomes harder and harder to obtain.

When you see problems occurring under your watch, do you jump right in and take charge or do you leave them for someone else to solve? Strong Leaders are problem solvers and know how to turn problems into opportunities. Creative Leadership often involves knowing when to solve a problem yourself and when to use it as a learning opportunity to teach and encourage your staff to become problem solvers.

Scenario

"I agree that all of our Salespeople are doing a good job Richard, but we have already invested quite a bit this year in new training. Do you really think sending some of them to that advanced sales training class next week is worth the money it will cost?, asked Alan, the owner of ABC Motors during his daily morning meeting with Richard his new Sales Manager.

"I understand what you are saying Alan, but we can never provide enough training, as a matter of fact I would like to attend with some of the Salespeople", replies Richard.

"Really, what do you think they are going to teach you that you don't already know? Plus why would we want to spend the additional money to send you, you are the Manager, this class is for Salespeople," Alan asks.

"It is more the idea of me participating in the workshop with our Salespeople. I want them to know that I support them, believe in continual training and I really want to know what they are being taught so that I can support the new ideas when we all return", Richard states with confidence.

Alan responds with a stunned look and states, *"Do you*

really want to spend the whole day with a bunch of Salespeople learning how to sell a car?"

"I will do whatever it takes to make my staff stronger, more confident and better equipped to do their jobs, and yes, I think I would enjoy being with them, learning some new ideas and possibly re-learning some of the ideas of the past I may have forgotten. This is our team and I am there Leader. So do I have your permission to sign up half the sales staff and myself for this class?"

With some reluctance Alan states, *"If it is that important to you, than yes, you can sign up yourself and some Salespeople for the class."*

This scenario clearly demonstrates some of the very important qualities a Leader must represent. Leadership is a quality trait and must be demonstrated at all times.

Not only does Richard want to learn some new ideas, but he wants to show his commitment and dedication to his staff by attending this upcoming sales training class with his Salespeople.

Just consider how his Salespeople will respond once they realize their Manager is going to attend with them, and his goal for attending is to learn along side of them and to make sure that the ideas that are great will be implemented.

How many times have we sent our staff to training classes, only to have them return all excited about some new ways to sell cars and have then been told by a Manager either, *"that idea is not going to work"* or *"that is not the way we do thinks here."* And under this situation that will not happen.

Richard is the kind of Leader that most of us would want to work for. We would work hard for him, be committed to him and most likely be very successful under his Leadership.

Be an active part of your team's growth and they will reward you generously with great results.

CHAPTER 10
HOW A LEADER CAN HARM AN ORGANIZATION

As effectively as strong Leadership can benefit a Dealership, poor Leadership can cripple and immobilize those who work there. Yet with all of the vast information available today on effective Leadership, there is little to be found on the composition of poor Leaders and the negative affects they bring to the picture.

Our modern understanding of Leadership has come primarily from the contributions Psychology and the Behavioral Sciences have brought to our modern Western world. Until the 20th Century it was largely assumed that brutality and control was an essential part of Leadership.

As we have already seen, Leaders are those who make decisions on behalf of an organization or a group of people. Just as quality Leadership enhances a company's growth and well being, the negative power of poor Leadership hinders its workers and their potential for success. Bad

Leaders make bad decisions and bad decisions produce poor results.

Poor Leadership stems primarily from a lack of competence and a poor moral character in those who lead. Sadly, bad Leaders, like the good, are built rather than born that way. Though often neglected in the study of Leadership, understanding what not to do can be just as critical as knowing what to do when it comes to building a strong, effective organization. Avoiding those things that will hinder productivity and growth are an important part of a Leaders job.

Those things that make for poor Leadership must be diligently discovered and rooted out if there is to be growing progress and profits within the Dealership. When poor Leadership is dominant within any organization, its ultimate failure is just a matter of time.

During my over twenty-five years working as a Sales and Motivational Trainer, I have learned many things; none more important than the value of effective Leaders and their ability to enhance our lives and careers. Those who depend upon their Managers to provided direction and guidance, also expect them to know how to handle the tangible things that make us successful.

If a Sales Manager fails to stay on top of things like a proper balance of new and used vehicle inventory, they hinder the ability for their sales staff to have the products needed to draw Customers and fulfill sales expectations. If a Parts Manager is not prepared to have available stock on hand that is commonly required, Customers will go elsewhere and profits will be diminished.

The many facets of Leadership requirements in the retail automotive business are complex and often specialized. Those Leaders who fail to keep abreast of the innovations and opportunities that can make a difference in the success of the Dealership will eventually disqualify themselves from Leadership.

In your quest to raise your own Leadership qualities to a high standard, it is imperative that you continue to make an honest assessment of both your positive and negative management practices. The strategies and qualities you will develop as you implement the principles in this Leadership book will greatly improve your career and life, and those of the men and women you supervise.

➢ How a Leader can harm an organization – When they think they have made it

Leadership can be misleading when it presents itself as the climax of a successful career. In most cases it is the beginning of a new and challenging role with more responsibilities and greater potential for failure.

Climbing to the top of any high peak is often a long and arduous journey fraught with struggle and potential hazards. In most cases trained guides are required who have made the trip before and know the way up. For those who make it, there is always a celebration when they reach the peak and breathe air that few mortals ever taste. But danger still lurks nearby.

Having fulfilled a goal that took years of dedication and discipline to reach, it is easy to get too comfortable and forget the danger that still lies ahead. A mere misstep and you may soon discover the downhill tumble to be faster than the climb up. And if you are tied to other climbers they are probably going down with you.

For successful Leaders the comfort zone often lies hidden within those things we looked forward to experiencing when we finally reached the top. Company car, big office, six figure salary, nice bonuses, and shares in the Dealership. Who would suspect that those very things that inspired you to make the sacrifices that took you to the top could eventually bring your dreams crashing down upon you?

When Leaders think they have finally made it, they become a hindrance to themselves, their team, and ultimately the entire organization. The very same momentum that got them to where they are as Leaders can stall when they think they have arrived. When that happens, new ideas, risk taking and innovation may be sacrificed for the safety of the comfort zone.

Like racers with no trophy or record to achieve, the comfort of the status quo can suck the momentum out of a team or a vision in no time. In a challenge free neutral zone no one will go for the gold.

Leaders who think they have arrived will follow the path of least resistance. They will protect their new safety and security by setting goals that are easy for them to accomplish. They will lose their momentum and drive, feeling there is nothing left to achieve. Leaders who fall victim to their own comfort zone may soon have to face the harsh reality that their Leadership is coming undone.

When the activities of Leadership cease, the title becomes nothing more than a masthead. If this happens a Leader will spend more time polishing their awards then training their staff for excellence.

Strong Leadership depends upon an internal drive that cannot be fueled by material things alone. It is driven by the personal satisfaction of continued growth and the never ending quest for personal excellence.

➢ How a Leader can harm an organization – When they think they know it all

When the Greek Philosopher Socrates was about to die, one of his disciples asked him what was the wisest thing he had learned in the getting of all his knowledge. To which the wise old sage responded, "That I know . . . that I know not".

Seeing that the Western world still bases most of its logic and reason upon the processes Socrates developed, it might behoove Leaders to revisit some of the things he taught.

When a Leader arrives at the place where 'his knowledge, is knowledge' they have cut off the potential for any further growth or innovation. There is little more frustrating than working with or for a Leader who thinks they know it all. It is the death knell of creativity, and causes all forward progress to come to a halt.

Leadership is primarily attained and sustained through the continuous search for new understanding and more effective ways to lead others. When someone thinks they know it all they become un-teachable. They can no longer guide others beyond where they have already led them. For any Leader to reach their full potential and continue to successfully lead others they must remain teachable.

Never mistake arrogance for wisdom. When a Leader thinks they know it all, they will lead their team in an endless circle of past accomplishments. They become little more than a Maintenance Manager. When past achievement becomes the model for future potential it puts a virtual freeze on growth in an organization. If that occurs, only new Leadership can break the ice to get things flowing again.

Leaders who become full of themselves will micro-manage those around them. They will reject new ideas and insist that their staff do what they say at all times. This not only frustrates team achievement, it causes stress and creates instability among employees.

Perfection is paralyzing. Yet the pursuit of excellence is a journey that requires constant forward movement. As Socrates pointed out, there is value in knowing what you know, but not as much as in knowing what you don't know.

Leadership is often like guiding a ship through a dense fog. If you are not careful you may end up where you have already been. When that happens it is hard to regain the momentum required to move forward.

➤ How a Leader can harm an organization – When they stop learning

As we look at the dangers of stagnant Leadership, we can clearly see that what *makes* Leaders strong is the same thing that *keeps* them strong. Nothing is more important to Leadership than continuing education. Great Leaders will maintain their desire to learn and grow even after they retire from their careers.

Leaders view life itself as a learning opportunity. They don't learn because they are Leaders – they are Leaders because they learn. Like the blade of a knife, Leaders know they must keep their cutting edge sharp. If they become dull, they are of little value to themselves or to those they lead.

Innovation requires that you as a Leader stay on top of your game in order to chart a course for success for yourself, your staff, and your organization. In a constantly changing industry like ours, off the shelf strategies will no longer carry the day.

As a Department or Dealership Manager, your people look to you for direction and decision making. They are busy carrying out the directives you assign then, and the daily goals they have for producing the required results. Like a Navigator on a ship, your ability to properly assess the currents, weather and tides of the business can be the difference between a successful journey or crashing your Dealership on the rocks.

The automotive industry depends upon the stability of things like market demands, vehicle finance availability, fuel costs, interest rates, tax incentives, shipping, credit availability, insurance costs and a host of other factors that must be monitored on an almost daily basis. On any given day, these things can set the pace or choke the potential for success in your business. If you as a Leader don't know what's going on around you, you cannot properly create the solutions needed to succeed.

Aside from the tangible things you are required to monitor and direct, you must keep informed of your team's activities, attitudes and well being in order to lead them to achieve the goals they have set for themselves.

Leadership is not for everyone. Those who choose to become Leaders must take responsibility for directing others and making decisions that can make or break everything they are trying to accomplish.

What you as a Leader do to stay on top of your game will decide what tools you have to lead and inspire others. To quote former President John Quincy Adams, "If your actions inspire others to dream more, learn more, do more and become more, you are a Leader."

Scenario

"I've waited a long time for this promotion," Don remarked, as he dusted off the shiny surface of his new General Managers desk at XYZ Ford. *"I was wondering if I'd ever get here. I guess they figured they had waited long enough to put the right man in charge,"* he said to Carl, the F&I Manager at the Dealership.

Carl had been with the Dealership quite a while too and he was hoping for this position, but he didn't let Don know how he felt. He knew it wasn't quite time to ask for any kind of raise or promotion yet until Don got settled in. As close as they were, he was pretty sure he could get some kind of play for that.

"Well from what I understand there's going to be a big shakeup and this is just the beginning" said Carl. *"They are planning to implement a lot of new training and want all of us to get on board with a new way of selling that the manufacturer is promoting. Are you ready to do all that re-training stuff?"*

Don gave a little chuckle as if he knew something that Carl didn't. *"I'll give it a couple weeks and things will be back to normal. Sure, I'll go to the training, but, in the end, you can either sell a car or you can't. That's the way I see it. I know this sales force and they'll get the job done like always. Once the economy picks up, everything will be just fine."*

Don looked at him with an air of self confidence. *"I've been in this business a long time. I've seen this 'new changes' stuff come and go. As long as I can get cars out the door and you can get them financed we'll both have plenty to be thankful for."* He leaned back in his new office chair smiling. *"I've put in a lot of years for XYZ Ford. It's about time I got some of the perks, don't you think? Besides, they wouldn't have made me the General Manager if they expected me to change the way I do business."*

"I hope you're right" said Carl. *"To tell you the truth though, it is definitely getting harder to deal with this new breed of Customers. They all come in with information under their arms and it's not that easy to sell the financial products we offer these days. Maybe it really is time to learn some new techniques."*

"Well I don't know about you Carl" said Don as he hung some of his achievement plaques on the wall of his new

office. *I don't think I need to learn new things. What I know got me this far and it will be just fine for the future."*

The chances of XYZ Ford seeing any effective changes taking place under Don's new Leadership are pretty slim. He obviously thinks he's arrived now and plans to set the cruise control in the 'status quo' position. He doesn't put a lot of stock in the new plans the Dealership has for growing their Customer base and he knows how to do what he has always done and thinks that's good enough.

If he convinces his sales force in the same way he is trying to convince Carl, they may all fake it for a while to please the Dealer and then revert back to the same methods they have relied on for years. If he is able to convince other Department Managers to agree with his outlook he will probably insure that XYZ Motors doesn't make any significant changes in the way they do business.

The problem is that Don doesn't really think he's doing anything wrong. He believes his outlook is right and he sees no need to investigate any new knowledge or processes to find out how to improve the business and become a great Leader.

Unless the organization is prepared to do whatever it takes to implement change, Don will probably win the battle and take the wind out of the sails of their new efforts to improve. His lack of visionary Leadership will eventually harm the organization in ways that prevent future growth and hinder them from reaching new levels of productivity and profitability.

CHAPTER 11
THE INVERTED TRIANGLE THEORY

Have you ever found yourself so busy doing what you do that you didn't have time to look and see if it was worth doing? We often hear of someone having a 'Wake up Call' that changes the way they view things. For me that happened at a company Christmas Party back some thirty years ago.

I had been working as a Sales Manager for a dealer group and it was time for our annual Christmas Celebration which was held every year for all of the Managers and upper echelon of the company. It was always quite a hullabaloo and lots of awards were given to Managers for exceptional achievement in their Department or their Dealership.

As the night progressed, I began to look back over the year and review the things that had been accomplished and suddenly it occurred to me: it wasn't the Managers or even the Dealer who made the year so successful. It was all the other employees who did the things they do every day.

The Salespeople, the service people, the people in parts, and the secretaries, receptionists, the bookkeepers, and administrative assistants; it was the drivers, the facilities workers, the lot attendants, the detail department and so forth. Without them, nothing would have been accomplished at all, none of us would have been there receiving these awards. And guess what? None of them were even invited to the party.

It was then and there that I gained a new understanding of what made a company successful. Out of that came my vision for 'The Inverted Triangle'. Let me explain.

In most company hierarchy diagrams, you have the Dealer who is President or CEO of the company on top and below them in descending order comes the Vice President, the CFO, the CIO, the General Manager, the Various Department Managers, the Assistant Managers and on down the line to the very bottom row where all the workers in sales, service, parts, facilities and office workers are.

Yet, I realized that if I were to ask any one of those important people at the party that night to sell a car, fix an engine or transmission, find a part for someone who needed one, or even work as a receptionist at the front desk, their answer would probably be a resounding . . . NO they could not do that!

It was clear to me that things were upside down in our understanding of what made the Dealership's successful. In fact many of those who were invited to the Christmas Party had never even met those who had worked so hard to make that party a success. They worked in the same company, but their positions isolated them to a certain level of relationship with staff and outside of those who were their peers or above, they had no knowledge of the others who worked at their Dealership's day in and day out.

When we invert the company triangle we can see the way things really ought to be. The Dealer, and all those who work in upper levels and Management should be the support system for those who directly interface with the Customers. Without the front line soldiers who make the deals and do the jobs that make everything work, there wouldn't be any Customers and therefore there would be no business.

And, thus, I developed the concept of the Inverted Triangle. Putting those who are normally at the bottom on the top, and those that are at the top on the bottom.

From that day on, I made a pledge to myself. I would do my best to honor those who did all the things that made my company successful, and get to know them as well as I could. I would make a point of regularly spending time with them, individually and corporately, and finding out who they were and what their dreams and aspirations were for their lives, their families and their careers.

After thirty years of keeping that pledge, I can tell you it was one of the best decisions I have ever made in my business life. Not only has it enhanced my company's success, but it has made a tremendous difference in my own life and career and in how I view those who work with me every day at David Lewis & Associates. And I hope it has done the same for those who work with me. In fact, I know it has.

As I mentioned earlier, I travel extensively and am usually out of the office more than I am there. But when I am there, I make it a point every week to take one of my employees out to lunch or dinner. Not my Managers, but what I call my line workers, my Salespeople, in-house trainers, software developers, technical support staff, office staff and even the part time people that work the phone making customer service calls and sales calls. And then when I am done, I start the cycle over again.

During that time I get to know them and how they are doing. I don't talk as much as I listen. I want to know how they are and how their family is doing. I want to know about their spouse and their children if they have them. How their children are doing in school and what aspirations they have in life. The more I know about them, the more I can appreciate them as a person and how they feel about the work they do at our company.

I ask about their personal life so I can understand what makes them happy and what motivates them to do what they do. The more I know about them the more I can help them reach the goals they have for their own lives and families.

Sometimes I will spend my first day back in town going from desk to desk speaking with each of them individually just to see how they are doing. I let them know what has been happening with me and some of the things that I am doing and how important their work is for helping me do my job well.

Aside from that, we sometimes have company gatherings with the families all together. This way we can all get to know each other better and enjoy our relationships outside of work. These have proven to be wonderful times for all of us and have greatly enhanced the quality of our working together.

When I travel and speak to Leaders I share my story of 'The Inverted Triangle Theory' and encourage them to think about how to implement its principles into their own company structure. Some are more open than others, but I always share it when I am teaching Leaders.

When we consider the things I have written in this book concerning the practice and characteristics of true Leaders 'The Inverted Triangle Theory' makes perfect sense. To understand and honor the work of those who are subordinate to us in our positions as Leaders is to actually validate our own Leadership. Not recognizing and rewarding the value that these workers bring to our business and our work as Leaders is a serious oversight on the part of any organization.

Try to imagine any profit without them. They are not just spokes in your organizational wheel; they are the spokes that hold the wheel together and give it the strength needed to move down the road to success. It is their work and dedication to excellence that brings Customers back to your Dealership for their next service appointment, replacement part, or vehicle purchase.

Take them out of the picture and you have a paved lot with cars sitting there gathering dust; a service department where no service is being done; a sales department without anyone selling your vehicles. You have Customers calling with no one answering the phone, or arriving at the Dealership with no one to meet them and introduce them to what you have to offer.

Can you now see the value of those who are often taken for granted or considered unimportant in the scheme of things? Think of the disaster that would fall upon your business without these people in it.

I highly recommend that you give serious consideration to 'The Inverted Triangle Theory' and how to approach its implementation into your Dealership structure. I assure you that you won't regret it and it will greatly alter the way you view those who work with you and how they view themselves and their place in your company.

It will also change the way Customers feel when they come to your place to do business. Remember, happy employees make for happy Customers. And after all, isn't that what we all want.

CHAPTER 12
THE DOWNSIDE OF A LEADERSHIP POSITION

In spite of the great benefits that go with the job, Leadership is not for everyone. Those who choose to become Leaders, must take responsibility for directing others and making decisions that can make or break everything they are trying to accomplish. Becoming a Leader is definitely not for the timid.

The personal challenges of Leadership require a confidence of self, and a commitment to excellence that separates the average from the exceptional.

For Salespeople in the car business the old adage was, "If they're buyers they're liars". The study of Leadership brings another idiom to mind: "Just because you're paranoid, it doesn't mean they're not out to get you."

Department Leaders must walk a delicate balance between compassion and control. They are often misunderstood in their intentions while trying to guide their staff. They sometimes find themselves navigating the lonely corridor that can run between their vision and that of upper management, all the while trying to inspire loyalty from both above and below.

As a Leader, if you are too strict in your application of Leadership you can weaken those you actually intend to strengthen. If too liberal, you may lose their ability to bring correction when it is necessary. On any given day, you may walk in the limelight and then suddenly find yourself thrust into the shadows. For Leaders, the trip from hero to zero can be as short as the next failed sales campaign that didn't reach its intended goal.

Are you still with me? If you are still smiling and enthusiastic at this point I have great hopes for you as a Leader. Genuine Leadership threatens the status quo and often calls for a leap into the unknown. Nothing is lonelier than Leadership, but nothing is more rewarding.

➢ Downside of a Leadership Position – A Leadership position sometimes is misleading

As we look at the downside of Leadership, I recognize the potential for you to stop listening to me thinking I may be talking about others, but certainly not you. You may instead choose to go about your business as usual, patting yourself on the back and thinking about your best month this year so far.

I myself am a Leader in my business as a Motivational and Leadership Trainer. What I am saying to you rings true with me also. When I point the finger at you there's a thumb pointing back at me. Because of this I take my research and training very seriously. I know that my own success as a Leader depends upon my implementation of the same principles and actions that I teach others.

Leadership can often be a very misleading occupation. It may appear to the newcomer as a position of authority that demands respect and obedience. But anyone who has been at it for a while recognizes that authority is most effective when it is used to serve others, rather than to serve oneself.

Most successful Leaders have a history of following someone who taught them their craft. Often it is a compilation of ideas and habits that were developed over time while working for other Leaders; not necessarily in a classroom setting, but often by on the job demonstration.

In the old paradigm, a business Leader was someone who had reached the pinnacle of their career after a long time of service to a company. But, Leadership can be misleading when it presents itself as the climax of a successful career. In many cases it is the beginning of a new and challenging role with more responsibilities and greater potential for failure.

Remember, as I told you in a previous chapter, Leadership is a verb, not a noun. The actions you take make you a Leader, not the position you hold. A Leadership position is in fact nothing more than the station from which a Leader carries on the activities required for creating success and helping others reach their intended goals; like a launch pad at Cape Canaveral where some have lifted off to far away places and new horizons, and others have crashed and burned at great cost and disappointment.

One of the great misconceptions about Leadership is that it stems from the gifting and natural talent of special individuals. Successful Leadership rests upon a commitment to excellence and a dedication to learning the craft of guiding others to accomplish a common task.

➢ Downside of a Leadership Position – Leaders who rely on their position often de-value people

As we have already seen, a position of Leadership can overcome those who are not prepared for it. Being an effective Leader requires far more than a name tag on an office door. Leaders who function from position only often see all successful outcomes as the direct result of their Leadership and may play down the contributions of their staff.

Those who view their position and authority as their source of influence see no further need to develop or grow new skills. If they do learn new things, they use them to control rather than to enhance the abilities of their team members. This hinders productivity and can effectively cripple motivation on the part of the staff.

As an effective Leader, the values that you hold for yourself and others are the standards that will keep you striving to learn and to walk transparently among those under your authority.

Suppose for a moment that you have come to count on your position to validate your Leadership. As you become more secure in your job title you will see no need to further your skills to get to the top. You are already there. Now imagine that some member of your staff continues to grow and develop their proficiency and understanding. As their Leader, they will look to you to guide them to the next level by reaching for higher goals and greater achievement. When this happens they may seem to you as a threat to your authority. You will begin to de-value their work and restrict their potential so as not to diminish your own value to those above you.

Strong Leaders recognize the significance of their co-workers and interact with those both above and below their station. Those who depend solely upon their positions become isolated and protective. If they do favor some staff members it will be based on loyalty to the Leader rather than on the quality of their work. This process causes rifts to develop among staff members as taking sides becomes a means of survival. When these things occur, it jeopardizes the workflow and negates the value of teamwork.

The eventual outcome of such Leadership is distrust and non-cooperation among team members. They will work more as independent employees rather than as an interdependent team guided by you, their Leader.

Walmart Founder Sam Walton once noted, "Outstanding Leaders go out of their way to boost the self esteem of their personnel. If people believe in themselves it is amazing what they can accomplish."

➢ Downside of a Leadership Position – Their title is more important than the role of the title

As an effective Leader, you are too busy guiding and implementing change to focus on your title. When the activities of Leadership cease, the title becomes nothing more than a masthead. If this happens a Leader will spend more time polishing their awards than training their staff for excellence.

As head of a Motivational and Leadership training company, I am on the road constantly working with others to develop quality in the Sales and Management staff of Dealerships. When I am gone the title on my office door still reads, David Lewis, President. If I have been an effective Leader, my team will function at the same performance level, whether I am sitting at my desk or on an airplane.

As a Leader, your actions define your role. Those who follow you will do so because of the inspiration and benefit they receive from your Leadership. When the title of Leader outshines the actions of your Leadership you are on a downward spiral to becoming a Boss and your ability to reclaim your Leadership is in jeopardy.

Remember, every time you take a step backwards and slide back into the Boss or Management role it takes three steps forward to get back your lost ground. When your Leadership role becomes more important than your actions, you have become a Boss again.

Again, and I realize I state this a lot, you must never forget that Leadership is a verb and not a noun. Those who lead by title see Leadership as a noun rather than the function of guiding and influencing others to accomplish specific goals and objectives. It is the difference between pulling a string and pushing one. A string being pushed goes nowhere, while one being pulled follows in the path of the one doing the pulling.

➢ Downside of a Leadership Position – They make good people feel weak

There is little more frustrating to a good employee than to work for someone who limits their opportunity for advancement. You may remember my story of a Manager I once worked for who never raised the bar above eighty cars a month. His inability to have a growing vision hindered my potential to become better at what I did.

Had I continued to work at that Dealership, I would still be selling to fulfill a 'get by quota', and he would most likely still be in charge. His lack of visionary Leadership made me feel weak, and I had to leave if I wanted to advance my skills and abilities to achieve more success.

No matter how much potential those under your supervision may have, unless you lead them toward excellence the ceiling for achievement will always be lower than what they could be reaching. You must inspire as a Leader or your staff will lack a channel through which their abilities can grow and produce.

My previous Boss was not a bad person; he just wasn't an inspiring Leader. Once his monthly goal was achieved he could see no need to stretch out and reach for higher objectives. Obviously the organization was similar in its ability to set a vision for him or he would have quickly been replaced as the Sales Manager.

Like a hot air balloon that has no source of heat, those under this type of Leadership can go no higher than the level they have already achieved. And like the balloon they will eventually head downward. A strong Leader creates strong followers. It is the nature of Leadership.

That doesn't mean that all of your team members will achieve to the same level once properly trained. But they will function to the best of their individual abilities if you know their goals and qualities, and work with them according to their specific potential. There is nothing wrong with a Salesperson who regularly sells twelve cars a month, if that is their true potential. But if they sell twelve and they are capable of selling twenty there is obviously something lacking in their motivation or in the guidance they are receiving.

It may be that this person's ability is being hindered by their perception of you as the Leader. If this person views you as an impersonal Leader, they will not seek your guidance openly. In this case you must implement actions to assure them of your support and commitment to their own goals. Leadership is much like a booster rocket. It must provide the initial force for moving upward, and only when a sustainable height and speed is reached can it release its payload to go on toward its intended destination.

➢ Downside of a Leadership Position – Leadership can be lonely

As a Leader, you must find ways to deal with the reality of isolation. The rise of the Coaching and Mentoring Industry over the past thirty years has in some way been the recognition of this problem. If you, as a Leader, have a way to regularly meet with other peers not connected specifically to your own Dealership this can help reduce the negative aspects of Leadership isolation.

Leadership usually demands some isolation, as over-familiarity breeds contempt. But having confidence in your team members will allow you to be transparent enough to avoid the extreme loneliness that can come with being the decision maker.

Some Leaders view their ability to work in isolation as a strength, and it certainly can be. When you have great confidence in your own direction and abilities you may choose to avoid too many outside ideas. You must however be careful to recognize that regular interaction with your team is required if you are to help them reach their goals. Your goals must be directly connected to theirs or your isolation may lead to loneliness.

Though often misunderstood, a Leader has one single outcome that validates his or her Leadership: Productivity. Style means nothing if it doesn't produce. Neither does gifting, personality, knowledge or past achievement. Having some form of accountability other than performance alone is essential for those who are in a Leadership position. Without it, they often make bad decisions because no one appears to be looking.

➢ Downside of a Leadership Position – If you fail as a Leader, the fall can be hard

In their newly released book, 'The Wisdom of Failure', authors Laurence G. Weinzimmer and Jim McConoughey write "*There is a paradox in Leadership: we can only succeed by knowing failure.*"

Though this may be true, it doesn't lessen the pain that Leaders experience when they fail. Getting back on the horse after a hard fall may not be so easy if the horse doesn't belong to you. Those who sit in positions of Leadership in automobile Dealerships have great performance requirements that go with the job; part of which is overseeing multimillion dollar floor plan inventories that must be sold in a timely manner in order to be profitable.

We often hear of sports team coaches and managers who get replaced if they have just one bad season. Our industry can be just as brutal, but it's not as visible to those outside of Dealership circles.

You too will likely experience failure at some time in your career, but know this: the distance of your fall can be greatly lessened by how many steps your ladder has on it. If you clearly outline your goals in short, medium and long term steps, and they are a part of a team objective plan, the probability of your catching potential problems before they become disastrous is much better.

It is also important that you develop a solid camaraderie with the people you lead. Those who do can often find a dependable source of support for the times when things don't go as they expected.

The truth is, it's not the fall that hurts it's the sudden stop. Leaders who operate in a vacuum experience this more than those who practice team development. Your willingness to be open and transparent in your Leadership can produce the type of staff that will absorb some of the blows of short term failures, and may even help cut them off at the pass before a tsunami develops.

Leadership that has never been tempered by failure is still walking in the shallow waters of limited potential. It is in the deep and rushing current of challenge and competition where true Leaders are born.

➢ Downside of a Leadership Position – Leaders are typically unrecognized heroes

As I have already mentioned, Leaders don't require a lot of patting on the back. For this reason they often do some great things without ever worrying about who gets the credit. Leaders are at the top of their game when they are solving problems and creating opportunities. They don't need to indulge in self adulation.

When an effective Leader is functioning at his or her best they make others look good. Those who are the recipients of what was accomplished often don't even know how much they contributed to the final outcome. It is not unusual for organizations and staff members to complain when things aren't going the way they want them to, but rarely do they thank or applaud the Leader when they are.

As a Leader, you will be expected to succeed at what you do. When things are going well under your Leadership, the fact that no one is complaining may be your best reward. Remember, strong Leadership isn't about the position you hold; it's about how you hold the position.

Every day we see heroes working in our service departments figuring out problems no one else could solve. No one takes them to steak dinner afterwards, and they don't expect it. They're just doing what needs to be done. They are Leaders in their own environment.

How many of us have had deals rescued by something done in F&I? It happens every week in most Dealerships.

When the Customer walks away happy, no one throws a party for the Finance Manager; they are just doing their job.

Leadership isn't always happening at the top either. Have you ever had an effective personal assistant who, as a gatekeeper, afforded you the time to deal with the necessary by taking care of little things demanding your attention?

Whether you're a Parts Manager making sure things get ordered as they should, or the Facilities Manager who keeps the Dealership clean and orderly so others can do their job well, what you do may often go unnoticed. It's the price of being good at what you do and making it easier for others to do their jobs.

As Ralph Waldo Emerson wrote, "There is no limit to what can be accomplished if it doesn't matter who gets the credit."

CHAPTER 13
SIGNS OF A POOR LEADER

Poor Leadership is an effect that can turn an otherwise excellent business into a mediocre enterprise. A poor Leader functioning anywhere in a company structure ultimately affects every part of the organization from the top down.

In today's business model, the successful Dealership depends upon a unique blend of interaction and interdependence. Because of this, it is important to assess the actions and attitudes of those in management, before looking at the general staff, whenever growth seems blocked or business is stagnating.

A quick tour of any American city today will take you past once flourishing Dealerships that are now empty, or near empty lots. Detroit itself looks more like a scorched earth policy has dominated the landscape than the once thriving City of Industry that drove our American economy in its heyday.

As the automobile industry adjusts to the rapid changes that are now taking place, a new style of Leader is also rising from the ashes. The age of the bureaucrat is making way for a new breed of Leaders who can adapt to the fast changing pace of today's information and technology based society.

If your Dealership is to flourish, you must be willing to provide Leadership that is well informed, flexible, tough, and ready to make the commitment required to navigate the hazardous waters of selling in a struggling economy.

Dedication, devotion and a commitment to success are all essential traits of a great Leader. Providing a good salary doesn't necessarily mean you are buying quality. Excellence comes from within and cannot be bought with a price. The willingness of Leaders to do what must be done dominates this new mentality.

Innovation is not only to be found in the material facets of our industry, but is now making its way into the marketplace of ideas. New ideals and processes that are geared to drive our business back into the forefront of the American economy are being tried and tested for their value and functionality. Leaders who are not willing to adapt to this new paradigm, will find themselves looking for work or picking up their unemployment checks.

To do this there must be a thorough understanding of what Leadership is in today's Dealership environment. As we move to establish the new paths we must push aside those old methods that elevate people to management who are not capable of providing the necessary Leadership for success.

➢ Signs of Poor Leadership – They leave on time (clock matters)

Today's Leaders are driven by the need to find a better way. The complexities of change require Leadership that can interface with the outside world to stay informed, yet work closely inside with their team members in order to guide their Dealership to achieve success.

The quest for excellence always requires going beyond personal convenience. When a Manager is more concerned about the time clock than meeting the daily goals they have set for themselves and their team, their Leadership is in question. As an effective Leader you must base your success on achieving what must be done rather than just putting in your time at the office until weeks end.

If you find yourself regularly leaving on time you are probably not doing your best and either have goals that are set too low or opportunities that are being ignored.

Anyone who knows the car business has learned the value of last minute deals. Managers who cut a deal short or put it off until tomorrow in order to be home for supper will set a precedent for their sales team that will produce mediocrity.

When I was in sales, I always appreciated a team member that would cover for me if a Customer of mine came in unexpectedly and I was off. I would do the same for others and we would split the deal. That's just the way it's done, and sometimes it can't be avoided and is definitely better than losing the sale altogether. But Salespeople who have a lot of split deals because they don't want to come in early or stay late to get the job done will never really consistently reach the top.

This same mindset applies even more so to those in management positions. As a Leader, your willingness to go the extra mile will inspire those who work for you to do the same. But if you stick to the clock, so will they. That doesn't mean that you slave away day in and day out just to keep your job. It just means you do what has to be done to reach your objectives, and when surprises or opportunities raise their heads you take care of them.

Time Management is an important key to Leadership. Leaders don't waste time. It is their most effective tool. If you find yourself looking at the clock to see if you can leave, it's time to re-motivate yourself with new and innovative ideas. If you stay on the cutting edge you will always be excited about what are you are doing.

Leaders don't get bored with their job because they are too excited about overcoming the obstacles that challenge their ability to do it well. They appreciate a job well done and are not satisfied with status quo results, either from themselves or from those under their Leadership.

➢ Signs of Poor Leadership – They rely on their employee rights

As we look at the signs of poor Leadership, certain things begin to stand out to help us identify weaknesses that need to be improved. If you have ever interviewed a potential employee whose first questions were about vacation, sick days and overtime pay, you have seen the mindset that kills Leadership potential.

When an employee is overly concerned about his or her rights, the likelihood of them ever being satisfied is very small. If you have worked in a union job you will see how easy it is to become self absorbed with employee rights. That doesn't mean they are not important, but Leaders never rely on such things to mobilize their interest or motivate themselves for peak performance.

Leaders who are focused primarily on their rights as an employee will lead in such a way as to benefit themselves above others. The organization, and their staff, will take a back seat as they serve their own self interest. If you go back and look at the qualities of a strong Leader you will see that self-serving is in direct contrast to what real Leaders do.

As a Leader, if you are overly concerned about your rights, you are already dealing with a sense of deprivation and dissatisfaction. This may indicate that you are not happy with your own performance and are looking for a way to justify that by focusing on what you are not getting from the organization. This can be perilous to your ability to execute good Leadership and will certainly bleed over to those who work for you.

Strong Leaders always have the rights of others in the forefront of their minds. They know too well that their own success depends upon that of their staff and this attitude drives their actions. By doing this, they provide their employees, their organization and their Customers with an outcome that will often exceed their expectations.

In my experience a great Leader will always excel. Anyone smart enough to own a Dealership is rarely stupid enough to drive away a good Leader by squeezing them in the area of money and benefits. If this is the case, it will become known and opportunities will abound for that person in other places.

➢ Signs of Poor Leadership – They do just enough to get by

If you saw the movie 'Amadeus' you may remember the scene where Mozart's sworn enemy Salieri is in a mental institution. As he speaks with a priest who had come to receive his confession, Salieri makes this statement about himself: *"I am the patron Saint of Mediocrity."*

Could there be anything worse than to conclude that your best efforts have consigned you to a life of mediocrity?

Successful Leaders know this is not really possible. True achievement is not ultimately measured by the result of what you attain; it is the quality of what you give to attain it that sets you apart. Poor Leaders, on the other hand, make an art form of getting by. They do just enough to keep the dogs at bay. The bar is always set for acceptable, and never raised to exceptional.

Some statements that identify poor Leaders may include phrases like, "At least we didn't go backwards this month." Or excuses like, "We're not doing any worse than the other Dealerships."

Poor Leaders are satisfied with minimal performance and lackluster results. They are only motivated by a sense of loss and usually only react when the threat of loss occurs. They then pass this threat on to their subordinates and expect them to bring the solution. But their poor Leadership has produced a team that is unmotivated so there is little chance of change that might make a difference.

The disease of mediocrity can gradually infect you as a Leader and will eventually spread to the entire organization. When that happens, the only cure is new and innovative ideas and strategies, or a change in Leadership. Poor Leadership is the result of mediocre standards, bad information and limited vision. Those who desire to achieve more must always have something in view that beckons them to give their best effort at all times.

Like Salieri, if we look at the greatness of others to define our own value, we may end up killing our own potential as he did in the end. Mediocrity, like Leadership, is a verb not a noun. It is defined by the lack of action, just as Leadership is by the quality of its actions.

As I said in a previous chapter, a strong Leader is like a good knife blade. They keep the edge sharp at all times.

I hope that is why you are reading my book. I am committed to do my best and give you tools to help you keep your blade sharp. I promise that I will never settle for less.

Scenario

"I look at things a little differently now than I used to Leonard," said Don, the General Sales Manager at XYZ Ford. *"When I first started in this business I was gung-ho like some of these young guys just getting started. At some point though you come to realize it's only a job and you can't sell your soul to it, know what I mean?"*

Leonard is the Used Car Manager at XYZ and has worked with Don for a few years. He is trying hard to convince his friend to start conducting some training at their Saturday morning sales meeting. He was hoping they could start role playing scenarios every week and help the Salespeople create personal word-tracks to help boost there sales.

"Those things really worked for us when we were in sales" said Leonard, *"but none of these guys have a clue about what it takes to truly sell a car. If there not lay-downs they don't know how to sell them."*

Don didn't mind having a training meeting, but not Saturday. He always stayed out late on Friday night and getting there by 9:00 every Saturday was hard enough, and then the thought of preparing a training session was not what Don wanted to do. *"I'll tell you what Leonard"*, Don replied. *"You seem motivated to do it. I'll let you conduct some training. Besides, we hit 100 units last month, what's wrong with that?"*

"Nothing, but I just think we can do better Don", said Leonard feeling a little frustrated now, *"I think you should do it though Don; you were always so good at these things and you are the General Sales Manager, shouldn't that be your responsibility?"*

"It will be good practice for you Leonard," said Don, *"Besides, the Salespeople all listen to you. They act like I'm untouchable or something. I'm just trying to keep a little distance. I think I should do that as a General Sales Manager so they won't get too comfortable with me and lose their respect for my position."*

"If you're sure you don't mind I'll do it," said Leonard, *"I just hope the Dealer won't have a problem though with me leading it instead of you though."*

Don gave him a bit of a sarcastic look and said, *"When's the last time you saw him here on Saturday pal? I wouldn't worry about that. And don't forget I don't even work every Saturday. As the GSM I can take every other Saturday off. No use wearing myself out."*

"OK, I would like to do it. Actually I think this new product line is great," Leonard stated. *"And I've been learning some new selling techniques and word tracks I would like to share with everyone, I think it can help us hit 120 cars this month."*

"Hey . . . don't get all 'Joe Girard' on me Leonard. Next thing you know you'll want us to start passing out flyers at the mall or advertising on Craig's List," stated Don with a chuckle. Leonard had a little laugh to himself too, as he had already thought about doing the Craig's List thing.

"Anyway Leonard," Don added, *"you have your little training thing on Saturday mornings and I'll pop in once in a while to lend you my support."*

At this point you have to feel sorry for Leonard. He's stuck working for someone who lost his motivation long ago. The trouble is Don is in charge and the Dealer is actually thinking about promoting him to GM at some point when the current one retires in a few months.

When Managers fall to this level they are on the slippery slope to mediocrity. His poor Leadership has infected the entire Dealership and his Sales Managers. Unless something happens to change things they will always be producing the bare minimum with little or no growth.

The biggest concerns for this Dealership will now be staff. How long are talented people going to stay working for someone who only thrives for mediocrity?

A true Leader would jump at the chance to motivate his sales force to more success; especially having someone like Leonard working with him who has a real vision for growth. But unfortunately Don has fallen into the trap of the Comfort Zone. Hopefully he will wake up before it's too late.

CHAPTER 14
STRONG/POOR LEADER STATEMENTS

Of all the tools Leaders use to motivate and empower their people, their words are the most powerful. The power of words to instill and evoke emotion is undeniable. History has clearly shown us that words can either destroy or empower a person's hidden potential.

The words and statements used by those in positions of Leadership can be powerful for the building up or the tearing down of their employees. Strong Leaders know the power of the tongue and they are careful to use their words to accomplish good things rather than to destroy.

➢ A poor Leader states: Do this or else

To a poor Leader, one of the most useful tools is the ultimatum. When your position affords you authority to command workers with a 'do this or else' mentality, you are only a few steps away from being a dictator.

How can someone under this style of supervision ever feel good about their work? They are too busy worrying about the loss of their job or trying to extinguish the negative feelings they have for someone who is supposed to be their Leader.

Of course the values of commitment, dedication, loyalty and devotion which I have presented in earlier chapters are meaningless to this type of Leader. Statements like this are meant to put someone in their place and to elevate the speaker above them. Words like these can deeply discourage someone and will never produce positive results.

Remember, one of the key benefits of pursuing effective Leadership skills is your exposure to new ideas and methods of communicating with others. Often, you will find that the simplest changes in verbiage and terminology can make all the difference in the world.

Think about how these two statements from your Service Manager would make you feel as a Service Writer in your Dealership:

"I've spent a lot on advertising this special so each of you had better sell fifteen brake jobs this month or else don't expect any bonus money."

(or)

"The money we spent on these new ads should bring in a lot of Customers who need new brakes. If we can reach our goal of fifteen brake jobs each this month we will all get a nice bonus."

The first statement is threatening, antagonistic and intimidating. The second is motivating, empowering and inclusive. Both present the same facts, but only one will encourage people to perform their job with excitement and enthusiasm. One gives them something to look forward to, while the other warns them of what to expect if they don't perform.

In your quest to become a better, more effective Leader, don't just accumulate new information and think that's all there is to it. Take advantage of every opportunity to implement what you have learned and establish an effective and encouraging method of communicating directives to your staff.

Your ability to effectively communicate goals and directives in a stimulating and motivating way can make the difference between your being a successful Leader or dysfunctional Boss.

➢ A poor Leader states: Because I said so

If you remember in my earlier discussion about Bosses, I said that they often view their workers as children that need to be constantly corrected. Whether or not this type of control method is right for children, it certainly has no place when dealing with adults in a workplace environment.

Leaders who use 'because I said so' to get things done are procuring for themselves a place of resentment in the minds of their employees. This type of condescension is demeaning and self-centered. Those who use such words reveal their arrogance and their inability to create an environment where true success can be realized.

Though this type of person may think this is the only way to enforce authority and make things happen, it never feels that way to those on the receiving end, I assure you. Breaking yourself free from utilizing this type of supervision is not easy, but it must be done if true Leadership is to take place.

Sometimes, people gain a position of authority because they appear to 'get the job done.' Owners or upper management who care little about their staff may employ someone like this hoping to avoid personal contact with their employees. To this type of Dealership, their Managers and Bosses are nothing more than drill sergeants.

Respect is a self perpetuating force. When you give it to someone it comes back to you in some way. Disrespect does the same. Leaders who disrespect their employees will be disrespected in return. Poor Leadership of this sort manifests itself in many ways, but almost always comes from personal insecurities masquerading as strength.

But here's the good news: just as strong Leaders are made not born, so it is with poor Leaders. And all learned behavior can eventually be unlearned by someone who wants to change.

The basic rule of thumb for all of us is this: Treat others like you want to be treated. Keeping this in mind at all times can only benefit and enhance your success as a Leader. You will never gain the high ground if your management philosophy includes demeaning communication to your subordinates.

Leaders who communicate with their staff with respect and dignity, will always receive a higher level of production than those who use demeaning and condescending language to enforce their authority.

➢ A poor Leader states: This is the way we do it

Relying on yesterday's methods to get today's results is a sure way to have more of the same tomorrow. In the land of 'this is the way we do it' who needs a Leader? Let's just do what we did yesterday and it should work out... right?

Maybe in the Land of Oz, but not in the real world.

Yet, some people still see this as a valid way to succeed. Nothing could be further from the truth. The business graveyard is filled with supervisors that followed that path to their own demise. If this is how you manage things in your Department or Dealership it's time to adopt a new system.

Leaders who rely on yesterday's methods as a model for today, only show their lack of motivation and inspiration. Not only in the inspiration they are giving to others, but that which they are receiving for themselves.

As I mentioned earlier, strong Leaders view their position as an opportunity to learn. Unless you are committed to the process of growth and change, you will always be stuck running plays that you ran before. Your Leadership must be *inspiring* to those you lead. But before you can be inspiring, you must be *inspired.* Your desire to learn and develop new and innovative methods and strategies will keep you on the cutting edge as a Leader.

The factors that made things work before do not exist today. Everything has changed. Today, we live in a service oriented society. Fifty years ago, it was all about product. What drives Customers today is altogether different.

Automobile advertisements once stated 0-60 in 6 seconds. Today's window stickers might read 35 MPG City - 40 MPG Highway. Fifty years ago you bought a car because of how *fast* it would go. Today, you buy one because of how *far* it will go on a gallon of gas. Everything changes and Leadership is no different. Keep up or move over. That's the way it works.

Innovative Leadership relies on the constant flow of new and proven information in order to excel in today's demanding business culture. In a time when information is king those who close the door on learning close the door on their future.

➢ A strong Leader states: Let's work together

Surely, by now you can see we are living in a time that demands our full attention to keep abreast of the changes occurring in our business today. The shift from individual endeavor to interdependent team Leadership has proven to be the most effective method for achieving maximum results.

If you recognize the need for transformation in your Department or Dealership there is never a better time to start than now; or a better person to start with than yourself. Strong Leaders know the value of getting the ball rolling in the right direction. That's why they are Leaders; they are not afraid of change. In fact, they embrace it! And why not? Who wants to carry the weight all by themselves? Since Newton discovered the Law of Gravity we've known about the power of leverage. Why have we waited so long to apply it to the practice of Leadership and Management?

Today, there is so much to know that one person can't know it all. It's the sharing of knowledge, talents, effort, and imagination that makes great things easier to accomplish. 'Let's work together' is the motto of today's great Leaders who are making a difference in our industry and in our world. And it's about time.

➢ A strong Leader states: I'll come to you

When America was coming out of The Great Depression, President Roosevelt delivered one of the most inspiring speeches of modern history. In his first inaugural address as President he said these words, *"The only thing we have to fear is fear itself."*

No doubt fear is a powerful force that often keeps people from moving into the unknown. But move there we must if the things that are blocking our progress are to be overcome.

The traditional lines that once ran between the employer and the employee have been all but eradicated in today's business culture. But those of us who are Leaders must take the first step. The employee cannot say to the Dealer or Department Manager, *'You need to change the way you do things.'* The first step taken must be downward from above; it cannot be expected to come up from below.

This is a great change from the days when Bosses built a platform for their desks so they could sit higher than those who sat before them. Today's Leaders see themselves as part of the whole rather than as the 'Big Boss Man' who does all the thinking. Those who are afraid to get their hands dirty will not do well in this environment.

As a Leader, you must welcome this change and provide innovative training and increased opportunity for those in your organization who desire to advance themselves. Working outside of the box has now become working inside, outside and all around it. Sometimes it means bringing in other new boxes altogether.

But those who work for you will not take the first step. You must go to them. They cannot get to know you until you make an effort to get to know them. You can start with Dealership functions where all employees see each other outside of the business. Sometimes seeing that your Boss is a human just like you can make a big difference.

Never underestimate the value that having fun together can bring to your organization. Things like company sporting teams and cookouts for the families are amazing for what they can do to promote team spirit. Once the walls are down everyone can roll up their sleeves and get back to the job of making a living for themselves and their families. Only now they are not doing it alone, they're part of a team.

Great Leaders don't stand safely on the hillside watching their armies fight the battle. They take up their own sword and join the fight alongside their troops, and so doing they inspire them onward to victory.

➢ A strong Leader states: What do you think

It is very interesting to see a workers reaction when a Leader first asks them for their opinion or advice. Usually they are at first surprised; then, after they realize you are serious they can often give an exceptional point of view.

Some Leaders don't believe their employees can think. They view them as mere robots who get paid to carry out the actions and ideas that come from the Leaders overflowing vault of knowledge and experience. Workers who are under this type of Leadership often carry out their tasks feeling no responsibility for its outcome. They just do what they are told. If it doesn't work out it can't be their fault since it wasn't their idea.

The old adage, "Ours is not to reason why, ours is but to do or die", may have worked well in the Charge of the Light Brigade, but Lord Tennyson wouldn't get very far with that in today's business environment.

If you want to bring all of your guns to the fight, you need to make sure you know what resources you have available in those who are on your side. You might be amazed at how much your workers know about their job, and yours. If you don't ask them though, they will probably never tell you.

As I mentioned before, my business takes me on the road quite a bit. I am usually gone most of the week when I do training in other cities and states. When I return to my office I like to take some time to speak with my employees to see how they are doing. I value their opinions of the work that we do, and I like to hear how they are doing both at work and at home. They know they can approach me if there are problems or issues that need to be addressed, and I trust them to carry on their work when I am not there.

Each person in my organization plays an integral part for which I have great respect and appreciation. Without them I could not do what I do to the best of my ability.

Leaders who come to know and value the ideas of those who follow them usually learn more about themselves in the process. And when the battle begins they move as one single unit.

➢ A strong Leader states: I'm here to help you

As we study the various character traits and actions of strong Leaders, it is important to understand the motives that drive them. The desire to help others improve and better themselves is central to the kind of Leadership needed in our industry today.

Becoming an effective Leader is one of the most valuable and challenging pursuits of life. What could be more exciting then to know that your work is helping others achieve their dreams and goals in life?

The new model for Leadership is not so much a Commander as it is a Coach or Mentor; someone who will get down in the trenches and demonstrate Leadership first hand. As this type of Leader you will inspire others to follow because they see in you the potential to accomplish something that is worthwhile; something that will benefit them and help them achieve success.

As someone in charge, you may have the authority to command action, but if those you lead lack the skills or knowledge required for the job, you will have little chance of reaching your objectives. With that in mind, the more you equip and empower your people, the better the chance they will be able to carry out your plans and objectives.

Strong Leaders learn to serve and to move things forward by motivating and inspiring others. They don't say *'I'm here to take charge'* but rather, *'I am here to help you.'* They know how to develop a vision, draw others into that vision, and lead them in the disciplines and processes that will bring about a successful conclusion.

In today's auto Dealerships, there is a new generation of young men and women who are seeking a career that will give them a positive foothold on the future. At a time when many college graduates are taking minimum wage jobs to survive, the automobile industry presents great opportunities for those willing to learn and develop the skills for this profession.

This creates a challenge to those in Management: how do we train them to become effective and successful, while remaining ethical, productive, and committed to excellence? The answer is simple: we must become teachers who share the knowledge we have learned to benefit and empower those who are now joining our industry. And we must do so by cooperative demonstration and not by verbal instruction alone.

By being a Leader who offers guidance and inspiration, your voice speaks stronger than those who shout commands from the Boss's chair. Your commitment to lead your team into new strategies and proven methods will make you an invaluable asset to your staff and to your organization.

➢ A strong Leader states: I know you can do this

The ability to inspire self confidence in those who work for you is one of the greatest qualities you can possess as a Leader. You must never be afraid to release those you have trained into the success they are able to achieve. Your willingness to empower your people with the type of knowledge and training that will lead them to success will be a key to your own path upward in your career.

As we have already seen, one of the negative aspects of the Boss character is that they limit the potential of their subordinates for fear of a threat to their own job security. Strong Leaders never do this. They know that the path upward for them is made more secure when those who take their place have the same goals and motivations as they have. For this reason, they take pleasure in empowering those they train to become Leaders themselves. Since their own success is measured by the achievements of those they manage, their Leadership is reinforced when those below them are promoted.

Nothing says Leader more than your ability to have confidence in those you have trained to complete the work you have trained them to do. Once you have empowered and equipped those you lead, have the confidence to believe in them and let them endorse your Leadership by their achievements.

Former President Theodore Roosevelt once said, "The best executive is the one who has sense enough to pick good men to do what he wants done, and self-restraint enough to keep from meddling with them while they do it."

As I said in a previous chapter, not all team members will achieve the same levels. In any team there are different personalities and talent levels. Your job as a Leader is to draw the best out of each, according to their abilities and your skills as a Leader.

When you encourage your staff and support them where they need your help, you establish their confidence in you as their Leader. You also empower them to believe in themselves and in their abilities to grow and achieve success. Your ability to inspire others to have confidence in you as Leader is a good thing. When you inspire others to have confidence in themselves, it is greater still.

➢ A strong Leader states: Let's think outside the box

Leaders march to a different drummer. They are not satisfied with yesterday's methods or results. They know that the key to success often lies ahead of them rather than in what worked at other times.

As a Dealer or Department Manager, it is likely that you have been to seminars or training sessions before where you were asked to connect a box made of nine dots with a single line without lifting your pen, or retracing the line twice. To do this you must go beyond the edges of the box to complete the puzzle successfully. This is often given as a demonstration for thinking outside of the box.

Today, thinking outside of the box takes on a whole new perspective in our industry as we are in some ways having to start with brand new boxes altogether. Since the shakeup of the economy, nothing is the same as it once was.

Some see this as a disaster, but for the strong Leader, this is an opportunity to rebuild in a new way that is in harmony with the changes that have occurred in a world now dominated by information technology.

Twenty years ago, most Dealers shunned the idea of selling cars online. *"No one will buy a car without a test drive"* they would say, *"they want to smell that new car smell."*

Today, any savvy Dealership not only sells cars via the Internet, but has added an Online Sales Department to their organizational structure. If there are still people working strictly in the old box they aren't selling as many cars as they could be.

In a press release in February of 2007, Auto Trader Magazine announced that a retail study of the company had found it was responsible for facilitating more than $99 billion in annual sales. This accounted for 28% of the 43 million used vehicles then sold yearly in the United States.

Since that study was completed, the auto industry shakeup and plunging economy has changed everything. But unless America becomes a Third World Country the auto industry will overcome the current challenges and rise to new heights. Americans not only want good vehicles, they depend upon them for their everyday life and business. It's the American way and this will not likely change any time soon.

As a Leader in your company, will you seize this as a time of opportunity? Will you look for new avenues and methods that will drive your business forward and upward?

It is not enough for you alone to think out of the box. Encourage your team members to do the same. Spend time evaluating your market and put your heads together. Develop new strategies that will put you on the cutting edge and drive Customers your way. This is the key to turning the challenges of our current world into opportunities for the future.

CHAPTER 15
EIGHT QUOTES TO PONDER

Throughout this book I have shown how the impact of specific events and the onward march of progress are changing our industry and those of us who work in it. As we have studied the retail automotive business through the eyes of Leadership, there are two things that stand out as necessary for success: *Change* and *Growth.*

I have painted a picture of the future that is both positive and challenging and I believe the future of our business can indeed be very bright. How bright depends upon how we meet the challenges ahead of us as Leaders.

There are eight things we as Leaders must consider if we are to see the success we all desire for ourselves and for this industry.

1. Become an agent of change – Always make bad situations good situations

Change is not only about where you are going, it is also about where you are coming from. Leadership that will not relinquish the past cannot embrace the future. By this I do not mean that the past is necessarily bad. But it may have little to offer in relationship with what is required to do the job today.

Of course some things never change. Good values and principles are the same today as they have always been. Integrity, loyalty, dedication, hard-work; these things never lose their significance or ever need to be changed. It is vision, and the implementation of resources and processes that must be reinvented to meet the demands of innovation.

Leaders believe in what others often consider impossible. This is how progress becomes reality. The question is never 'Will things change?' but, 'How will things change, and who will be the agents that set the necessary change in motion?'

History shows us that if it can be imagined, it can be achieved, and as I have demonstrated over and again throughout this book, Leaders don't fear change, they embrace it. They know that if nothing changes things eventually go backwards, and they are willing to step up and do what is required to make the changes required for forward movement.

Rarely, will business organizations put forth the effort and expense required for effective transformation until they have to. When things are bad it takes Leadership to turn things around and make them better.

Becoming an *Agent of Change* is an essential part of your job as a Leader. You must envision change, promote change, implement change and oversee its processes. To do this successfully you must totally believe in its outcome and invest yourself in acquiring the knowledge and training necessary to ensure change will achieve the desired objectives.

You must make sure your positive goals are not hindered by negative attitudes. Those who work with you must have confidence in your Leadership, as well as in their own abilities. Because it must be done, you must believe it can be done! Because it can be done, you must believe it will be done!

But, remember, in most cases it won't be done unless you do it. And when it is successful, others may get most of the credit. It is the price of true Leadership and it has always been this way.

2. Just because you are appointed a Leader does not mean you should stop growing as a student or as a Leader

Leaders often do not receive the credit for what they have done. This never stops a true Leader from doing what they do best: being a Leader. What motivates Leaders is never the final outcome. That is merely the target for which they aim in order to reach their current objective.

Because strong Leaders love to learn and grow, when they reach the top they usually take a deep breath, enjoy a brief respite in the sun, and then look for the next mountain they plan to conquer.

The great World War II General George Patton said, "It is only by doing things other's have not that one can advance."

As a Leader, you must be willing to go where others will not go. In order to do this you must be willing to learn what other Leaders know. The quest for knowledge and understanding always marks the path to great Leadership.

I encourage you to stay on top of your game by constantly seeking to improve your knowledge and skills as a Leader of others. The resources available today are countless and the only thing that can stop you is you.

In this book, I have presented many aspects of a Leaders role and of Leadership as a whole. I have shown you the philosophy of Leadership as well as its history and its various forms and applications. But, you must put these principles into action before they can produce results.

No matter how good your abilities are or how much potential this information has to help you grow, it is your implementation of these ideals and practices that will solidify your Leadership.

Being a Leader does not mean that you will automatically launch out every time you need to. The temptation to take the path of least resistance will always be there beckoning you to dim the lights and relax. That little voice saying, "Haven't you done enough?" will softly whisper from your comfortable office chair and tell you to give it a rest.

It is then that you must shake yourself by the back of the neck and plunge into your next set of goals. If you find yourself lacking in new ideas, dive into the goals of your individual team members and help them with theirs. It is only when the pot is being stirred that things will rise to the top. Leadership must be active and growing in order to function as a force for change.

3. Always change the me to we

Can you imagine a Dealership where everyone there thought only of themselves and what was best for them? As a Leader you must instill in your team the knowledge that they are part of something bigger than themselves. You do this by the way you speak and through how effectively you perform your Leadership role.

If you say, "We are a team and I really need your help," yet reject any ideas that team members bring to the table, they will soon perceive you are not genuine in what you say.

If Leadership is about helping others reach their goals, make sure that you listen when those you lead want to express their ideas, views, or opinions. If your staff members don't feel valued by you, they will never share what they really think, or give any input they may have to offer. You must let them know that you depend upon them as much as they depend upon you.

Interdependence is only real when those who practice it are dependable. This goes for you as a Leader as well as for those you lead. If you are not dependable, you cannot expect that of them.

One of the simplest ways to encourage this form of team spirit is to practice verbiage that exchanges the word 'me' for the word 'we'. This can only be natural if you indeed feel that way about your team and your position as Leader.

Do you really believe in your staff and their contributions to your department or your Dealership's success? If so, make sure you let them know it. When those you lead feel that their contributions are important and valuable, they will take ownership of your objectives and do their best to help you accomplish them.

4. Interaction fuels action

Goals and objectives are the fuel for high achievement. So it is with the interaction of your team and the actions you desire to implement. Like the huddle in a football game before every play, there's something that happens when people put their heads together to form a plan.

As a Leader in your Dealership, you are the quarterback calling the plays. But as quarterback you depend upon the advice of your coaches and team members in order to move the ball down the field toward the goal line. Once the agreed upon play is chosen your players will take their place on the scrimmage line, eager to get the job done.

The excitement and stimulation that takes place when you are a part of something bigger than yourself is always amazing to behold. As a Leader, your willingness to interface with your team members, and to have the shared experience of reaching your goals together, is like fuel that fires your team for action. Every individual action takes you closer to the goal line that you have set, and each person's part is critical to the ultimate victory.

But don't forget! Your team will not come to you, you must go to them. It is your responsibility to set the interaction in place as a part of your Leadership. This includes individual as well as team communications.

Because each of your team members has different motivations and personalities, you will need to know these things in order to effectively communicate with each one. Your group interactions will be different and must target the goals of the team rather than those of the individual.

An important part of your Leadership is to be attentive to how each member is meeting their daily goals. If they are falling behind or are not attempting to fulfill them, intervention must not be delayed.

Make sure you know what their goals are and help them to be realistic in those they set for themselves. They must be achievable or they will fail to succeed. This can set them on a downhill slide that can affect the entire team morale as well as the projected outcome.

Team Leadership is only effective when it takes into consideration the abilities and the personalities of those being led. These can only be discovered through consistent and open interaction.

5. Progress requires change

As the Quarterback you know that no matter how good your last play was, when it is over the ball moves to another scrimmage line. You must constantly monitor the progress of your team and make decisions for changes in strategy when things aren't working. Your ability to do this can make the difference between winning and losing.

You must learn to read the effectiveness of your team as they implement your plays, and be always ready to make the necessary changes that will get things going in the right direction.

Don't allow things like attitudes or personality conflicts among team members go unheeded. Things like this can have a snowball effect that can bring progress to a standstill and even shipwreck your plans.

Remember, strategies and methods are just tools and not to be taken personally. If something is not working, no matter how much you have put into it or like it, you must change course.

Like a coach, you must be constantly learning new ways to accomplish your objective. You must be fearless in your quest to discover new approaches to win and to become a more effective Leader. You already know this if you are a Sales or F&I Manager in your Dealership. That's why there are so many options available today to help buyers get the best choice for their purchase.

There are factory incentives that can make a vehicle more affordable, leases that can often work better than a purchase. There are reduced prices on certain inventory, used car versus new car prices, college incentives, seniors incentives, previous buyer incentives, and special interest rates. The list goes on, and on.

These are all options that you can put into play in order to make something work for the Customer to finalize the deal. They are tools in your bag as a Coach and Leader.

Just as you wouldn't hesitate to use any of these to benefit the Customer and make the deal, neither should you overlook the potential changes available to help you reach your goals in Leadership. A wise Leader, like a football quarterback, must know when to pass, handoff, kick or run the ball. All the while he is looking downfield to see if there's an opening that can bring his team closer to the goal.

6. How do you make an organization better? Invest in the people who work there.

Anyone who has run their own enterprise before, knows the importance of investing back into their business. Without that, companies cannot progress and grow. In our business, Dealers constantly have to upgrade equipment in the Service Department, invest in new inventory, and remodel the facility to make it more attractive.

Yet it is not always easy to know where best to invest when it's time to grow. Should I increase the advertising, enlarge the facilities, open another location, buy more inventory? All of these things come into play in business.

Though all of these are important for sure, there is nothing more valuable to your Dealership than the investments you make in the people who work for you. It is people that win a Customer's business, not just product, advertising, or a beautiful Dealership.

This is something the most successful companies in the world know. That's why when you go to a Walmart there is always a smiling Greeter to meet you at the door with a welcoming word. The Greeters job is simply to make you feel better about shopping there, and it works. Have you ever seen a Walmart that wasn't busy all day long? It's amazing how a smiling face can even make spending money feel better.

In 2009, during a down turning economy, American companies spent over $125 billion on learning and training programs for their employees. Why? Because they knew what had the most potential for turning business back in the right direction. In the same way, the money you invest in the people who work for you will make all the difference in the success of your Dealership.

Some Dealerships think that if they flood the floor with hungry Salespeople this is the way to go. But listen, one professional who is well trained and motivated can do more than five people who are just there taking up floor space. How you invest in your staff is the best indicator of how much you value what they do. It is also the clearest sign that you understand what motivates people to do business with you.

Leaders know that the training and work environment you provide for you staff is as important as the money they earn. You can't buy quality but your investment in your people can create quality in them.

7. Organizations get better when the people get better

The Online Business Dictionary says an organization is: *"A social unit of people, systematically structured and managed to meet a need or to pursue collective goals on a continuing basis."*

Let's look at the key words in this definition:

people, structured and managed to pursue collective goals on a continuing basis."

This definition alone shows us how the condition of the organization depends upon the condition of its people. It also defines the purpose for this book about Leadership. My goals is to help you as a Leader *develop your people, structure and manage them around a set of collective goals*, and to do so *on an ongoing basis*.

As a Leader in your Dealership, the best thing you can do for the organization is to develop your people to the highest level of efficiency, professionalism, and excellence possible. The investment you make toward these goals is well worth it and has been proven to make all the difference in those companies who have seen the benefits of this policy.

Your workforce is the first contact that Customers have with your business. Whether it's the Receptionist on the phone, the Service Writer in the drive through, the Salesperson on the lot, or the Management team in the office; how they handle their part of the Dealership package is how people will perceive your organization. If you've ever been to a lot where none of these things mattered, you would quickly see what I am talking about.

As I have said repeatedly throughout this book, all of this starts with you. It is your commitment to the quality of your people that will produce high standards in your organization. Strip the Dealership of its workforce and all you have is a nice building with lots of vehicles and tools for service.

It's the people who work there that make all the difference. Without them nothing gets sold, nothing gets serviced, nothing gets done at all. The best organizations have the best people, because the best people are what make them the best organizations.

8. The test of Leadership occurs when you are not there

It is appropriate for me to end the book with this topic because it is the test of how well you learn to apply the methods, ideas and principles found on these pages.

Have you ever seen a movie where the parents go on a vacation or business trip and leave their home in the care of their high school aged children? They lay down the rules and get all the assurances from their kids that they don't have to worry. As soon as they board the plane the party starts and everything goes haywire from there.

Can there be any more disappointing experience for parents than this? I don't think so.

Just the same, what happens when you are gone from the Dealership is the test of how well you have trained your people. If the qualities and disciplines you have instilled in them have born real fruit they will continue with business as usual, or even excel. If not, they will default to their previous condition and reveal the weaknesses of your Leadership as well as their own character flaws.

Effective Leadership duplicates itself in the people who are being led. It produces a quality in the team members that is not only embodied in the Leader but radiates from the entire team.

There is always a natural hierarchy that develops among staff that is often unspoken, but clearly understood. If this has been properly developed your presence doesn't leave when you're gone, it just transfers to the next Leader. Team members will naturally look to the most qualified and effective person in line when they need assistance if you are not there. If that occurs they won't miss a beat, nor will your authority and Leadership be compromised.

Leadership is a transforming power. It doesn't exist by rules and regulations, but is a force for change that affects people in a permanent way. The things we learn, good or bad, from the Leaders in our life, always stay with us.

Nothing can be more fulfilling to you as a Leader than for the training and learning you have passed on to your staff to take deep root and make a permanent difference in their lives and careers. If you have done your job well don't be surprised to find out that your people have exceeded your expectations and made you proud while you were gone.

The greatest prize a Leader can receive is when those they have led emulate the things they have taught them in their own lives. For me, I have no greater joy than to learn that the things I have taught others are producing fruit that is making their work and their life better and more successful.

CONCLUSION

I hope that you have benefitted from our journey into the world of Leadership. Never has there been a more crucial need for Leaders in our industry than at this very time. As we attempt to turn the corner from an extended period of economic and industry upheaval in North America, I believe that the key to our success is to be found in strong and effective Leadership.

This book was not created from research done in libraries, bookstores or online. Since 1986 I have travelled throughout America and Canada training Salespeople, Department Managers, and Dealers in the principles that you have found on these pages.

My first book, 'The Secrets of Inspirational Selling' received a great response from people in our industry and has further revealed the growing need for quality Leaders who will guide our Dealerships in the coming years.

Kenneth Blanchard, author of the highly acclaimed book 'The One Minute Manager' once wrote, "*The key to successful Leadership today is influence, not authority.*" With this I wholeheartedly agree.

It is the affect of the influence one has on those they lead that validates their Leadership, not the authority that is granted by their position in the organization. If it is good it will produce good results. If it is bad, the results will be unsatisfactory and unproductive.

There was a time when someone's Leadership was defined by how many people served under them and the perks and privileges granted by the position they held. Today's Leaders understand that their success is best realized by empowering those who are subordinate to them and helping them reach their own success goals.

In our own time, the emergence of the self-help industry has given average people the ability to learn and develop step by step processes that can lead to successful achievement in any field of endeavor. Today, those who will commit themselves to absorb and implement the advanced resources available for the willing student can realize great success outside of the University or traditional training methods.

In the end, Leadership is about people. It's about giving people what they deserve and teaching and guiding those who deal with our Customers to do just that. It is recognition that those who come to our Dealerships to spend their money on our products and services deserve the best we have to offer. The best in products, the best in service, and the best in Customer care.

Here's the wake up cry coming from today's Customers: *"If you don't do it. I'll find someone who will! And I can because today I have the information I need to help me do it."*

In some ways, this may frighten some in our business. In reality, it's the best thing that ever happened to us. It forces us to do the right thing. Something we already should have been doing. And in truth, some of us already were. It is from this pool of genuine Leaders that I learned the principles I have shared with you in this book.

My travels have brought me face to face with every kind of Leader in our business. Every mile I traveled and every seminar I taught brought me closer to the reality of the need for a new breed of Leaders to man the helms of our Dealerships.

I hope you are one of those who will take what I have written and apply these methods and principles to your position as a Leader in your Dealership. If you do, I know you will find your own life and career, and that of those you work with, will benefit by your commitment to excellence.

I'd like to hear from you as you progress through the process of learning the things presented here. If I can help you in any way, or if your dealership would like to sponsor a *Leadership Management Seminar* in your area, please contact me or visit our company website for additional information.

Our web address is: www.davidlewis.com

Thanks again for taking the time to read my book and for making the commitment to become the kind of Leader we need today in our industry.

David Lewis

dlewis@davidlewis.com